SCRIPTURE AND CHRISTOLOGY

A Statement of the Biblical Commission with a Commentary

JOSEPH A. FITZMYER, S.J.

PAULIST PRESS
New York/Mahwah

IMPRIMI POTEST
Jacobus A. Devereux, S.J.
Praepositus Provinciae Marylandiae

NIHIL OBSTAT
Rev. Walter J. Burghardt, S.J.
Censor Deputatus

IMPRIMATUR
Rev. Msgr. Raymond J. Boland
Vicar General for the Archdiocese of Washington
July 18, 1985

The *nihil obstat* and *imprimatur* are official declarations that a book or pamphlet is free of doctrinal or moral error. No implication is contained therein that those who have granted the *nihil obstat* and the *imprimatur* agree with the content, opinions, or statements expressed.

Library of Congress Cataloging-in-Publication Data

Bible et christologie. English.
    Scripture and Christology.

    Translation of: Bible et christologie.
    Includes bibliographical references and indexes.
    1. Jesus Christ—Person and offices—Addresses,
essays, lectures.   2. Bible—Criticism, interpretation,
etc.—Addresses, essays, lectures.   I. Fitzmyer,
Joseph A.   II. Catholic Church.   Pontifica Commissio
Biblica.   III. Title.
BT202.B429   1986   232   86-2438
ISBN 0-8091-2789-X (pbk.)

Published by Paulist Press
997 Macarthur Boulevard
Mahwah, N.J. 07430

Printed and bound in the United States of America

CONTENTS

ABBREVIATIONS

AAS	*Acta apostolicae Sedis*
AB	Anchor Bible
EBib	Etudes bibliques
GCS	Griechische christliche Schriftsteller
JBC	R. E. Brown, J. A. Fitzmyer, and R. E. Murphy (eds.), *The Jerome Biblical Commentary* (Englewood Cliffs, NJ: Prentice-Hall, 1968).
NTS	*New Testament Studies*
QD	Quaestiones disputatae
RB	*Revue biblique*
SBT	Studies in Biblical Theology
SC	Sources chrétiennes
TPQ	*Theologisch-praktische Quartalschrift*
TQ	*Theologische Quartalschrift*
TS	*Theological Studies*
ZTK	*Zeitschrift für Theologie und Kirche*

FOREWORD

This book presents in a slightly revised form my translation of the Biblical Commission's recent document on Christology, on which I have also written a brief commentary. Details about the document, *Bible et Christologie,* and its publication will be found on pp. 1, 54. My translation and commentary originally appeared under the title, "The Biblical Commission and Christology," in *Theological Studies* 46 (1985) 407–79. With the kind permission of the editor, the Rev. Walter J. Burghardt, S.J., it is being reproduced here in book-form.

In this form I have included an English version of the preface of *Bible et Christologie,* penned by Henri Cazelles, P.S.S., who has recently been named Secretary of the Biblical Commission. Because of the length of my article in its original form this preface was omitted. In it Cazelles states the purpose of the Commission in issuing the document and calls attention to nine additional texts that were published in the original along with the document itself. In the original they are labelled as "commentaires," but they are not really commentaries on the document. They are independent essays on topics related to Christology. Anyone who is interested in them will have to consult the original publication.

Though I am presently a member of the Biblical Commission, I was not such at the time when this document was composed by the Commission and voted upon by the members. So I translate it and comment on it as an outsider.

Another English version of the Commission's document on Christology has meanwhile been prepared by M. J. Wrenn and published under the title "Bible and Christology," *The Wanderer* 118/11–14 (March 14,21,28 and April 4, 1985) 8–9, 10–11, 9, 10–11.

Several persons have assisted me in the work of my translation and commentary, and I should like to express my gratitude to them here. I am indebted in various ways to Walter J. Burghardt, S.J., Leo A. O'Donovan, S.J., and Thomas M. King, S.J. Needless to say, I am solely responsible for any inadequacies that may still exist in my text.

I should also like to record here that this is the first book that I have been able to produce on a word-processor acquired by my Georgetown Jesuit community with the aid of a substantial grant from the Loyola Foundation Inc. of Washington, DC. I am grateful to the members of that Foundation's board who positively considered the application that we had made.

I am likewise grateful to the Rev. Kevin Lynch, C.S.P. and to other members of the editorial staff of Paulist Press, especially the Rev. Lawrence E. Boadt, C.S.P., for their help in producing this work in book-form.

Joseph A. Fitzmyer, S.J.
Department of Biblical Studies
The Catholic University of America
Washington, DC 20064

PREFACE OF THE
SECRETARY OF THE COMMISSION

It is not the function of the Pontifical Biblical Commission itself to engage in exegetical work. The mandate given to it is to promote biblical studies in a correct and proper way and to provide worthwhile assistance to the Church's magisterium. Having been asked about biblical teaching concerning the Christ-Messiah, it has no intention of composing a document destined directly for biblical scholars or specialists in exegesis, or even for catechists, who have their own proper responsibility.

To promote an understanding of the Bible and to aid pastors in their mission, the Commission considers its task to be:

1. To carry out a careful examination of present-day studies in biblical Christology in order to reflect their diverse orientations and different methodologies and not neglect the risks that the exclusive use of some one methodology runs vis-à-vis a comprehensive understanding of the biblical testimony and of the gift of God given in Christ.
2. To present a summary of what the Bible affirms:
   a. in the Prior or Old Testament about God's promises, the gifts he has already bestowed, and the hope of God's people about a future Messiah;
   b. in the New Testament about the faith-understanding that Christian communities finally arrived at concerning the words and deeds of Jesus of Nazareth, understood in the light of those texts which Jewish communities had already come to acknowledge as of divine authority.

The Commission has deliberately left to a properly exegetical, literary, and historical investigation the study of the gradual composition of the biblical writings in order to concentrate on the testimony that has been arrived at in the canon of Scripture. Hence the title of this document: *Scripture and Christology*.

But it has also seemed useful to present pastors with some further treatment of the themes that the official document has only sketched. Certain members of the Commission were asked to compose additional texts, which they would publish on their own authority, but which the Commission would make use of in its common work. In those texts the reader will not find properly exegetical studies, fitted out with technical footnotes, but rather theological syntheses or biblical methodologies bearing on disputed topics in Christology.

Henri Cazelles, P.S.S.

INTRODUCTION

The Pontifical Biblical Commission has recently issued an extensive document on Christology. It is entitled *Bible et christologie,*[1] with a preface by Henry Cazelles, P.S.S., professor of Old Testament at the Institut Catholique de Paris, even more recently named the secretary of the Commission.[2] The text is issued in two languages, Latin and French, and it occupies 48 pages in each language. I have learned from Fr. Cazelles that the Latin is the official text, but that the French was the working text. Since there is apparently to be no official English translation of this important document, I am offering here my own private translation of it in view of writing a brief commentary on it, as I did in the case of the Biblical Commission's Instruction of 1964, "On the Historical Truth of the Gospels."[3]

A few preliminary remarks have to be made about the translation that follows. No English translation of this document is going to be entirely satisfactory; it has to be studied in the two languages for any serious understanding of it. Though the Latin and French texts are substantially the same, the differences between them are numerous. At times they are minor and need not be of concern; but at times the nuances are important. My English translation is based on the official Latin text, which is sometimes clearer than the French because of the case endings.

---

[1]Paris: Cerf, 1984; p. 294. The book also contains nine "commentaires," which are really not commentaries on the document but independent essays on Christological topics written by individual members of the Commission and (according to the book's preface) published on their own authority.

[2]Appointed on November 10, 1984; see "Vatican Bulletin," *Osservatore romano,* English edition 47/861 (November 19, 1984) 2.

[3]See "The Biblical Commission's Instruction on the Historical Truth of the Gospels," *TS* 25 (1964) 386–408. It can also be found in a revised form in my *A Christological Catechism: New Testament Answers* (Ramsey, N.J./New York: Paulist, 1982) 97–140.

But sometimes the French text, being more original, is superior to the Latin and clearer because of the use of articles, which Latin does not have. I have, therefore, kept my eye on the French text as well and have frequently supplied important variants in footnotes (L = the Latin text; F = the French text). Emphasis is supplied in the two texts, sometimes by italics, sometimes by quotation marks, and sometimes by both. Since the emphasis is not uniform in both, I have decided to follow one or the other, depending on the situation, and have often simplified the emphasis. Anyone who may be concerned about this aspect of the text will have to consult the originals. Both the Latin and French texts use capital letters for nouns in great abundance; since this is not usual in modern English style, I have invariably used lower case, except for titles that call for upper case. The text is difficult to understand, both in Latin and in French, because of the disregard of the sequence of tenses within paragraphs. I have done my best to reflect the sequence of tenses of the Latin, which disagrees at times with the French. So the reader should be cautioned from the outset that, if something seems strange in the tenses within a paragraph, the original texts should be consulted. It should also be kept in mind that the Commission often speaks of ''Scripture(s)'' when it means the Scripture(s) that Jesus used, i.e. the Old Testament. Lastly, I have at times added a word or a phrase in parentheses for the sake of clarity in English.

TEXT: SCRIPTURE AND CHRISTOLOGY

Many people today, especially in the West, readily admit that they are agnostics or nonbelievers. Does this mean that they show no interest in Jesus Christ or his role in the world? It is clear from studies and writings that are being published that this is scarcely so, even if the way of treating this question has changed. Yet there are (also) Christians who are deeply disturbed either by the variety of ways of handling the problem or by solutions proposed for it. The Pontifical Biblical Commission is anxious to offer some aid in this matter to pastors and the faithful in the following ways: (1) by presenting a brief survey of such studies to point out their import and the risks they run; and (2) by setting forth summarily *the testimony of Scripture itself* about the expectation of *salvation* and of the *Messiah,* so that the gospel may be rightly seen against its antecedent background, and then by showing how the *fulfilment* of such expectation and promises *in Jesus Christ* is to be understood.

PART I
A SURVEY OF METHODOLOGIES USED TODAY
IN CHRISTOLOGY

Chap. 1—A Brief Overview of the Approaches

There is no question of setting forth here a complete account of the studies of Jesus Christ. Attention is rather being directed to various approaches used in such studies. These approaches are summarily described in categories that make no pretense at a logical or chronological order, and the names of certain authors, who are the principal exponents of them, are mentioned.

3

1.1.1. The "Classical" or Traditional Theological Approach

1.1.1.1. This approach is used in speculative dogmatic tracts that present a doctrine systematically worked out, beginning with conciliar definitions and the writings of Church Fathers—the tract *De Verbo incarnato* (cf. the Councils of Nicaea, A.D. 325; Ephesus, A.D. 431; Chalcedon, A.D. 451; Constantinople II and III, A.D. 553 and 681) and the tract *De redemptione* (cf. the Councils of Orange, A.D. 529; Trent, sessions 5 and 6, A.D. 1546, 1547).

1.1.1.2. The tracts so worked out are enriched today with many elements introduced by the progress of modern research:

(a) Normally they make use of *biblical criticism* so that the data of individual books or of groups of books are better distinguished. As a result, their theological exegesis rests on a more solid basis (e.g. J. Galot etc.).

(b) Under indirect influence of a theology centered on salvation history (*Heilsgeschichte,* see 1.1.6 below), the person of Jesus Christ is more firmly anchored in the disposition of means of salvation called by the Fathers the *oikonomia* (or dispensation) of salvation.

(c) Given the different aspects from which theological questions are viewed today, some questions already well developed in the Middle Ages have been recently examined anew, e.g. the "knowledge" of Christ and the development of his personality (e.g. J. Maritain etc.).

1.1.2. Speculative Approaches of a Critical Type

1.1.2.1. Some speculative theologians think that the *critical reading,* which has brought so many advantages[4] to the field of biblical studies, must also be applied not only to the works of the Fathers and medieval theologians, but even to the definitions of the councils. These very definitions have to be interpreted in the light of the *historical and cultural context* from which they have come.

1.1.2.2. From the historical investigation of the councils it is clear that their definitions are to be regarded as attempts to overcome scholastic controversies or differences of opinion or ways of speaking that

---

[4]F: positive results.

divided theologians among themselves, even when all of them were desirous of reaffirming the faith that stems from the New Testament. Yet those attempts did not always fully overcome the conflicting views. When the cultural context and the language of acknowledged formulas are subjected to critical scrutiny, e.g. those of the Council of Chalcedon (A.D. 451), the *object* of the definitions can be better distinguished from the *formulas* used to express it correctly. But once the cultural context changes, the formulas can easily lose their force[5] and their effectiveness in another linguistic context, in which the same words do not always keep the same meaning.[6]

1.1.2.3. Formulas of this sort, then, have to be compared anew with the basic sources of revelation, with special attention being given to the New Testament.[7] Hence, some investigations about "the historical Jesus Christ"[8] have led certain theologians (e.g. P. Schoonenberg) to speak of his "human person." But would it not be better to speak of his "human personality," in the sense in which the scholastics used to speak of his "individual" and "singular human nature"?

1.1.3. CHRISTOLOGY AND HISTORICAL RESEARCH

Still other approaches proceed with the methodology of scientific history. Since this methodology had already proved its worth in the study of ancient texts, it was suitably applied also to the texts of the New Testament.

1.1.3.1. From the beginning of the nineteenth century, studies have, in fact, concentrated on *the historical reconstruction of the life of Jesus*—what sort of person he seemed to be to the people with whom he lived—and on the consciousness that he might have had of himself. Disregard of Christological dogmas was readily adopted by rationalistic writers (e.g. Reimarus, Paulus, Strauss, Renan, etc.). The same disregard was picked up by so-called "liberal" Protestants who wanted to substitute a critically established "biblical" theology for a "dogmatic" theology, which seemed to them to exclude all positive investigation (cf.

---

[5]F omits *vim suam.*
[6]F: the same words would no longer be used in the same sense.
[7]F: in returning with more sustained attention to the NT itself.
[8]F: the historical Jesus.

A. Harnack, *Das Wesen des Christentums*). However, this inquiry into "the historical Jesus" led to such conflicting results that the "Life of Jesus research" (*Leben-Jesu-Forschung*) finally came to be regarded as an unsuccessful undertaking (A. Schweitzer, 2nd ed., 1913). On the Catholic side, even though M.-J. Lagrange firmly established "the historical method"[9] in the study of the Gospels (*La méthode historique*, 3rd ed., 1907), the same difficulties were actually avoided only by postulating the integral "historical" truth of everything, even the most minute details found in the Gospel texts (thus: Didon, Le Camus; with some slight nuancing: Lebreton, Lagrange himself, Fernández, Prat, Ricciotti, etc.). The approach of R. Bultmann (see 1.1.8 below) found its starting point in the impasse which the "Life of Jesus research" seemed to have reached.

1.1.3.2. Since that time the "historical method" has been enhanced with new and important features. Historians themselves have been calling in question the "positivistic" conception of objectivity in historical study.

(a) This sort of objectivity is not the same as that in the natural sciences, since it has to do with *human experiences* (social, psychological, cultural, etc.), which occurred once in the past and so cannot be fully reconstructed. If, then, one would lay bare the truth about them, it could only be done by recourse to vestiges and testimonies related to them (monuments and documents). Yet one gets to the truth about them only to the extent that those same experiences are somehow understood "from within."

(b) The attempt to do this necessarily brings a certain amount of *human subjectivity*[10] into the investigation carried on. This element is sensed by the historian to be present in every text that recounts events or depicts the authors of events,[11] without prejudice to the value of the testimonies so preserved.

(c) *The subjectivity of the historian himself* is mingled with his work at every step, as he inquires into the "truth" of history (cf. H. G. Gadamer). For he treats the matter under investigation according to the aspects which most attract his own attention and interest. There is a certain

---

[9]F: firmly posited the principle of the historical method.
[10]Both L and F use the plural, *subiectivitates humanas; subjectivités humaines*.
[11]F: *en évoquent les personnages*.

"preconceived view" of them (*Vorverständnis*) that he has to adjust little by little to the testimony of the texts he is studying. Even though he scrutinizes and judges himself[12] in the course of such a contact, it rarely happens that he sets forth the conclusions of his study without them being conditioned by his own view of the meaning of human existence (cf. X. Léon-Dufour).

1.1.3.3. The historical study of Jesus is the most obvious example of this situation in which historians find themselves. *It is never neutral.* Indeed, the person of Jesus has an impact on all human beings, even on the historian—because of the meaning of his life and his death, the import of his message for human existence, and the interpretation of his person attested in different New Testament writings. The circumstances in which every study of this question is carried on explain the great diversity of results arrived at by either historians or theologians. No one can study and present in a completely "objective" way the humanity of Jesus, the drama of his life crowned in death, or the message he left to humanity in his sayings, deeds, or very existence. Nevertheless, *this sort of historical investigation is quite necessary* that two dangers may be avoided, viz. that Jesus not be regarded as a mere mythological hero, or that the recognition of him as Messiah and Son of God not be reduced to some irrational fideism.

1.1.4. CHRISTOLOGY AND THE HISTORY OF RELIGIONS

1.1.4.1. Another element has emerged that extends the basis of historical investigation, viz. "the history of religions."[13] It studies the contacts at work among religions. Must not one adopt this mode (of investigation) to understand, e.g., how the transition was made from *the gospel of God's kingdom,* such as Jesus preached according to the Gospel texts, to *the gospel of Jesus the Messiah and Son of God,* found in texts setting forth in diverse form the faith of the primitive Church?

1.1.4.2. Beginning with the nineteenth century, *the comparative study of religions* underwent a great development, and old approaches in this area of study were given new impetus. The two causes for this

---

[12]F has only one verb, *il se critique lui-même.*
[13]L: *scientia religionum;* F: *la science des religions.*

development were: first, the recovery of the literature of the ancient Near East, as a result of the decipherment of Egyptian and cuneiform inscriptions (Champollion, Grotefend, etc.); second, the ethnological investigations of so-called "primitive" peoples. From this it became clear that the phenomenon of religion could not be simply reduced to other human phenomena (cf. R. Otto, *Das Heilige,* 1916) and that it was made up of very diverse elements, in both beliefs and rites.

1.1.4.3. At the beginning of the twentieth century, the History of Religions School (*Religionsgeschichtliche Schule*) tried to explain[14] not only the origin and growth of the religion of ancient Israel, but also the rise of the Christian religion. The latter began with Jesus, a Jew living in the Hellenistic world fully imbued with syncretism and gnosticism. R. Bultmann unhesitatingly adopted this syncretistic premise in his attempt to explain the origin[15] of Christological language in the New Testament (see 1.1.8 below). The same premise is commonly admitted by those who do not espouse Christian faith. But when that premise is admitted, Christology is deprived of all substance. Yet the latter can be preserved without the denial of the value of the History of Religions.

1.1.5. THE APPROACH TO JESUS FROM JUDAISM

1.1.5.1. *The Jewish religion* is obviously the first to be studied so that the personality of Jesus may be understood. The Gospels depict him as one deeply rooted in his own land and in the tradition of his people. From the beginning of this century Christian scholars have cited many parallels between the New Testament and the writings of Jewish authors (cf. Strack-Billerbeck, J. Bonsirven, etc.). More recently, the literature from Qumran and the recovery of the ancient Palestinian targum of the Pentateuch have reopened questions and spurred on the study of these areas. Earlier, it was often the concern of this sort of study to shed light on the historical value of the Gospel texts. Today, however, the effort is rather to recognize better *the Jewish roots of Christianity,* that its in-

---

[14]F adds: in a genetic and evolutionary fashion.
[15]F: the formation.

dividual character[16] be more accurately described, without any neglect of the trunk from which it has sprung.[17]

1.1.5.2. After the First World War some Jewish historians, abandoning a centuries-old animosity—of which Christian preachers were themselves not innocent—devoted studies directly to the person of Jesus and to Christian origins (J. Klausner, M. Buber, J. G. Montefiore, etc.). They sought to bring out *the Jewishness of Jesus* (e.g. P. Lapide), the relation between his teaching and rabbinical traditions, and the unusual character, prophetic or sapiential, of his message that was so closely tied up with the religious life of the synagogue and the temple. Certain borrowings were investigated either in Qumran literature—by Jewish historians (Y. Yadin etc.) or by persons quite alien to Christian faith (Allegro)—or in the liturgical paraphrases of Scripture (targums)—by Jewish authors (e.g. E. I. Kutscher etc.) or Christians (R. Le Déaut, M. McNamara, etc.).

1.1.5.3. Some Jewish historians, turning their interest and attention to "brother Jesus" (S. ben Chorin), have set in relief certain lines of his personality; they have found in him a teacher like the Pharisees of old (D. Flusser) or a wonder-worker similar to those whose memory Jewish tradition has preserved (G. Vermes). Some have not hesitated to compare the passion of Jesus with the Suffering Servant, mentioned in the Book of Isaiah (M. Buber). All these attempts (at interpretation) are to be accorded serious attention by Christian theologians engaged in the study of Christology.

1.1.5.4. However, some Jewish writers (e.g. S. Sandmel etc.) are inclined to attribute to Saul of Tarsus aspects of Christology that transcend the human image of Jesus, especially his divine Sonship. Such an explanation is close to that of scholars of the History of Religions School (*Religionsgeschichtliche Schule*), even though it does not neglect the profoundly Jewish character of Paul himself. In any case, such studies of Judaism with all its variety in the time of Jesus are clearly a preliminary and necessary condition[18] for the full understanding of his personality and for the comprehension of his role in the "*oikonomia* of

---

[16]F: the originality of this one.
[17]F: on which it has been grafted.
[18]F: a necessary preamble.

salvation" that early Christians have attributed to him. Moreover, this is the basis on which a fruitful dialogue between Jews and Christians can be initiated, apart from all apologetic concern.

1.1.6. CHRISTOLOGY AND SALVATION HISTORY

1.1.6.1. In the nineteenth century some German Protestant theologians (e.g. J. T. Beck, J. C. K. von Hofmann), in order to offset either liberal "historicism" (see 1.1.3.1 above) or the idealistic monism derived from Hegel, which then enjoyed no little vogue, adopted the idea of "salvation history" (*Heilsgeschichte*). This idea was somewhat similar to what the Church Fathers and medieval theologians called the "*oikonomia* of salvation": when the gospel is heard with faith, *meaningful events* are found in human affairs, in which God has put, so to speak, traces of his intervention—events by which He has been directing history to its fulfilment. These events even make up the very texture of Scripture itself;[19] and the "consummation" of history understood in this way takes on the name of "eschatology."

1.1.6.2. Under the heading of "salvation history," Christology manifests diverse forms according to the idea on which the whole treatment is based.[20]

(a) As in (other) works devoted to the *New Testament titles of Christ* (cf. F. Hahn, V. Taylor, L. Sabourin, etc.) or to Christ as "the Wisdom of God" (A. Feuillet etc.), O. Cullmann has worked out on the basis of such titles an essentially "functional" Christology that prescinds entirely from "ontological" considerations of a metaphysical sort. The titles in question are either those used by Jesus of himself, intimately connected with his deeds and his conduct, or those that preachers of the gospel attributed to him in the New Testament. Such titles denote either the task carried out by him in his earthly life, or the task being accomplished by him at present in the Church, or the last, eschatological task toward which the final hope of the Church is oriented. Such titles also have to do with his pre-existence (P. Benoit). Thus soteriology (or the theology of redemption) becomes part of Christology itself, in a way that

---

[19]L: *tramam;* F: *la trame même de la Bible.*
[20]F: according to the point of departure chosen to construct it.

differs from the classical theological tracts that separated them, one from the other.

(b) W. Pannenberg starts out from the fact of *Jesus' resurrection* and considers it as the anticipation (or "prolepsis") of the end of all history. Since he holds that the truth of this fact can be proved by historical investigation (*Historie*), he thinks that the divinity of Jesus is demonstrated in this way.[21] His treatment of the life and ministry of Jesus takes its starting point in this conviction: Jesus' preaching inaugurated God's kingdom among human beings; his death brought them salvation; and by his resurrection God has confirmed his mission.

(c) J. Moltmann adopts from the outset *an eschatological perspective:* all human history appears to be turned toward a certain promise.[22] Those who accept this promise in faith find in it the source of a *hope* that is oriented toward the gaining of "God's salvation." This salvation, however, ought to have an impact on the whole of human existence in all its aspects. Indeed, this impact was already found in the prophetic promises of the Prior Testament. These promises the gospel now fulfils as it announces the death and resurrection of Jesus. For by means of the cross the Son of God took (upon himself) human punishment and death[23] so that in an unexpected way he might make of them the instrument of salvation. Moved indeed by love, Jesus became one who shared humanity burdened with sin and sufferings that he might free human beings in every way, whether in their relation to God, or in their psychological life (anthropology), or in their social life (sociology and politics). In this way the theology of redemption necessarily leads to a program of action. A similar concern is also found in "social exegesis" (cf. G. Theissen, E. A. Judge, A. J. Malherbe, etc.).

1.1.7. CHRISTOLOGY AND ANTHROPOLOGY

Under this heading are grouped various methodologies that have as a common characteristic a starting point in *diverse aspects of human experience or of anthropology.*[24] In their own way these methodologies

---

[21]F: at the same time he thinks that the divinity of Jesus is firmly established.

[22]F: all human history in its entirety seems to be polarized by a promise.

[23]F: at the cross, God took on in His Son human suffering and death.

[24]F: different social aspects of human experience and of anthropology.

reopen questions debated in the nineteenth century and the first part of
the twentieth about the "signs of credibility" that lead to faith. Such
studies began with the examination of external signs (classical apologetics), or with religious experience generically considered (the "Modernist" endeavor), or with the intrinsic exigencies of human "action"
as such (M. Blondel). In the meantime these problems have undergone
various changes; and the changes have influenced the study of Christology.

1.1.7.1. *P. Teilhard de Chardin* presented humanity as "the final
branch"[25] of evolution in the whole universe. Jesus Christ, as the incarnate Son of God, is thus considered as *the unifying principle of all
human history and of the whole universe* from its very beginning. So,
by his birth and resurrection the meaning of the entire "human phenomenon" is fully disclosed to those who believe.

1.1.7.2. According to *K. Rahner,* the starting point of Christological reflection is to be sought in *human existence,* in what he calls its
"transcendental" aspect: this consists basically in knowledge, love, and
freedom. These aspects of existence, however, find their full perfection
in the person of Jesus, in the course of his earthly life. By his resurrection, by his life in the Church, and by the gift of faith granted by the
Holy Spirit to those who believe, Christ makes it possible that the perfect
image and goal of humanity are realized, which without him could never
be brought to realization.[26]

1.1.7.3. *H. Küng,* concerned about the present-day conflict between the Christian religion and other world religions and various forms
of humanism, concentrates his study on the *historical existence of the
Jew that was Jesus.* He examines the way in which Jesus took upon himself the cause of God and that of humanity; then the sad events that
brought him to his death; and finally the mode of life of which he was
the promotor and initiator and which does not cease to flow in the
Church, thanks to the Holy Spirit. Hence, Christian conduct is seen as
a "radical humanism" that gives human beings real freedom.

1.1.7.4. *E. Schillebeeckx* so studies *Jesus' personal experience* that

---

[25]L: *"fruticem finalem"*; F: *le "bourgeon terminal."*
[26]F: *il rend possible à tous la réalisation du projet humain qui, sans lui, aboutirait à
un échec.*

he sets up a connection and a link[27] between Jesus' experience and the common human experience, and first of all with that of the people who were his companions in his lifetime. The death that Jesus underwent as an "eschatological prophet" did in no way put an end to their faith in him. The announcement of his resurrection, understood as a divine ratification of his life, shows that the same people recognized in Christ a sign of God's victory over death and a pledge of the salvation promised for all those who would follow him in his Church.

1.1.8. The "Existentialist" Interpretation of Jesus Christ

A similarly anthropological approach to Jesus is found in the "existential" (or "existentialist") interpretation proposed by R. Bultmann, exegete and theologian.

1.1.8.1. As an exegete, Bultmann picks up on the negative results to which the "liberal" Protestant studies of the life of Jesus had come; such studies, he maintains, can in no way constitute the basis of theology. Together with those who adhere to the *History of Religions School,* he agrees that the faith of primitive Christianity originated in a syncretism: Jewish elements, especially those which grew strong in apocalyptic milieux, were mingled with pagan elements coming from Hellenistic religions. As a result, the "Jesus of history" is separated as far as possible from the "Christ of faith" (according to the principle proposed by M. Kähler at the end of the nineteenth century).

1.1.8.2. Nevertheless, Bultmann wants to remain a faithful Christian and sets himself a truly *theo*-logical task. In order to protect, however, the authority of the gospel "kerygma," which has been preceded by the way in which Jesus conducted himself before God, Bultmann proceeds to reduce this message to *the proclamation of forgiveness extended by God to sinners.* This message is signified by *the cross of Jesus,* the genuine "word" of God inscribed in a historical fact. In this the message of Easter is contained; to it, indeed, one must respond with "a decision of faith" (cf. S. Kierkegaard). Such a decision alone offers a human being the possibility of entering with security[28] into a new and fully "au-

---

[27]F has only one noun, *à jeter un pont entre.* . . .
[28]F omits the adverb *secure.*

thentic'' existence. Yet this faith as such has no doctrinal content; it belongs to the ''existential'' order in that it consists in a pledge of ''freedom'' by which a human being commits himself entirely to God.

1.1.8.3. According to Bultmann, the ''mythological'' language of the period has been used to express the Christological and soteriological formulations found in the New Testament. This language, he says, has to be ''demythologized,'' i.e. interpreted, with due respect for the laws of mythological expression, so that an *existential interpretation* may emerge. The purpose of such an interpretation is that not only the practical consequences of the gospel message may come to light, but also the ''categories'' on which the structure of a ''saved'' human existence depends. In this regard Bultmann's reasoning depends heavily on the philosophical principles set forth by M. Heidegger in *Sein und Zeit*.

1.1.8.4. In his exegetical work Bultmann, no differently from his contemporaries M. Dibelius and K. L. Schmidt, goes beyond classical literary criticism and turns to the critique of the literary ''forms'' that have contributed to the ''formation'' of the texts (*Formgeschichte*). The aim of such (critical) study is not so much to derive from the Gospel texts the historical truths themselves about Jesus as to establish the connection between those texts and the concrete life of the ''primitive community,'' by determining their setting and function (*Sitz im Leben*), in order to uncover in a vivid way the diverse aspects of faith in the same community. However, students of Bultmann himself, though they have not rejected the principal studies of their master, have nonetheless sensed the need of situating Jesus himself at the outset and origin of Christology (E. Käsemann etc.).

1.1.9. CHRISTOLOGY AND SOCIAL CONCERNS

1.1.9.1. Since human existence depends on life in society, a number of ''readers,'' theologians and others, preoccupied with practical problems of social life, have turned their attention in particular to Jesus. While observing, or even experiencing themselves, the evils of human societies, they have recourse to *the ''praxis'' that Jesus followed* to find there an example that can be applied to our age. In the nineteenth century some Socialists, called ''Utopians'' (cf. Proudhon), had already devoted studies to the social principles of the gospel. Even K. Marx, though he completely rejected religion, was nevertheless indirectly influenced by

biblical messianism. F. Engels, in accord with his theory of "class struggle," proposed an interpretation of the hope of primitive Christianity
such as is found, for instance, in the Book of Revelation.

1.1.9.2. In our times exponents of various forms of *liberation theology,* which have been worked out especially in Latin America, are
trying to find in "Christ the liberator," whom some historians have depicted as a political opponent of the Roman empire (cf. S. G. F. Brandon), the foundation of a certain hope and "praxis." To bring a social
and political freedom to human beings,[29] as they say, did not Jesus *espouse the cause of the poor* and rise up against the abuses of authorities
who were oppressing the people in economic, political, ideological, and
even religious matters? Theologies of this sort, however, take different
shapes. For some of them, the necessary liberation has to embrace all
human affairs,[30] among which is included the basic relationship of humans to God (e.g. G. Gutiérrez, L. Boff, etc.). Others concentrate
mainly on the social relations of human beings among themselves (e.g.
J. Sobrino).

1.1.9.3. Furthermore, some Marxists, even though atheists, seek
for a "principle of hope" (E. Bloch) and consider the "praxis" of Jesus,
based on brotherly love, as a way open to the eventual emergence in
history of a new human society, in which integral "communism" will
find its perfect form (e.g. M. Machoveč).[31]

1.1.9.4. There are also readers of the Gospels who admit in principle the interpretation of social phenomena and human affairs proposed
by contemporary Marxists, who subject the writings of the New Testament to the analytical methods of this school, and who set forth *a ma-
terialistic reading* of them. In this way they deduce from such writings
principles of a certain liberating "praxis" that is, according to them, so
uninvolved in any "ecclesiastical ideology" that they may base on it
their own social activity (F. Belo). Certain groups of scholars, some of
them sincere Christians, have recourse to this method to join theory and
action, without, however, necessarily pursuing the theoretic goals of
"dialectical materialism."

---

[29]L is garbled: *Ut liberationem socialem et politicam hominibus afferatur* (with main
verb in a past tense).
[30]F: to stress the global character of the liberation needed.
[31]F: to cause to emerge in history.

1.1.9.5. Such modes of "reading" (the Gospels) center all their attention on the "historical" Jesus. According to these views, Jesus as a human being supplied, indeed, the starting point for a certain new, liberative "praxis"; and this mode of action must be reintegrated into the world of today, with the aid of new methods and means. In a way these attempts at interpretation take the place of what in classical theology were regarded as the doctrine of the redemption and social ethics.

1.1.9.6. From a notably different point of view some studies have emerged today that are aimed at a *practical theology*. They are concerned with social and political questions and seek to offer human beings, especially the poor and oppressed classes, a hope that is real and that can be realized: through the cross of Christ, God has made Himself an intimate member (*sodalem*) of suffering humanity to bring about its liberation (cf. J. B. Metz). In this way a transition is made to the ethical domain.

1.1.10. SYSTEMATIC STUDIES OF A NEW SORT

1.1.10.1. Under this heading are grouped two syntheses, in which *Christo*-logy is understood as a *theo*-logical revelation of God Himself. One comes from K. Barth, the other from H. U. von Balthasar. In each synthesis the more recent results of biblical criticism are not neglected; each one makes use of the entire Bible to present a systematic synthesis. Jesus of Nazareth and the Christ of faith are merely two aspects intimately joined to make up *the self-revelation of God* in human history. This revelation is clearly disclosed and made evident only *through faith* (K. Barth).[32] According to H. U. von Balthasar, the "kenosis" of Christ, manifested in his absolute obedience to the Father, even unto death on the cross, reveals an essential characteristic of the life of the Trinity itself; at the same time it brings about the salvation of sinful humanity, as he undergoes the experience of death for it.

1.1.10.2. According to K. Barth, Christ's entire existence takes on meaning only from the fact that he is the supreme *Word* of the Father. In communicating this Word through His Spirit in His Church, God opened the way to an ethic that demands of those who believe an in-

---

[32]F: This revelation makes itself clearly known only in faith.

volvement in the affairs *of this world,* even in those of a political nature. But according to H. U. von Balthasar, who advocates a contemplation of God by a mode that he calls "esthetic," rational reflection, historical investigation, and the involvement of human liberty governed by love coalesce in the very mystery of Easter itself. In this way a *theology of history* is sketched out that avoids the too restricted conclusions of Idealists and Materialists.

1.1.11. CHRISTOLOGIES "FROM ABOVE" AND CHRISTOLOGIES "FROM BELOW"

1.1.11.1. Among the above-mentioned Christologies, those that begin with "the historical Jesus" seem somewhat like Christologies that proceed "from below." On the contrary, those that concentrate on Jesus' relation to God the Father can rightly be called "Christologies from above." A number of contemporary writers try *to combine both aspects.* Beginning with a critical study of the (New Testament) texts, they show that the Christology *implicit* in the words of Jesus and in his human experience forms a certain continuum and is profoundly united with the different Christologies that are *explicitly* found in the New Testament. Yet this bond of union is discovered in very different ways (e.g. L. Bouyer, R. Fuller, C. F. D. Moule, I. H. Marshall, B. Rey, Chr. Duquoc, W. Kasper, M. Hengel, J. D. G. Dunn, etc.).

1.1.11.2. Although the approaches and the conclusions of these authors are far from being in agreement, the two following principal points are common to them:

(a) One must distinguish, on the one hand, the way Jesus *presented himself to his contemporaries and was able to be understood by them* (his family, opponents, disciples); on the other, the way those who came to believe in Jesus understood his life and his person *after the manifestations of him as one raised from the dead.* Between these two periods there is, indeed, no interruption;[33] nevertheless, an *advance*[34] of no little importance is noted, consistent with the early views,[35] and it is to be regarded as a constitutive element of Christology itself. This Christol-

---

[33]L: *interruptio*; F: *coupure*.
[34]L: *progressio*; F: *transformation*.
[35]L has *cum primigenis sententiis congruens,* which is missing in F.

ogy, if it has to take into account the limits of the humanity[36] of "Jesus of Nazareth," has to acknowledge in him at the same time "the Christ of faith," fully revealed by his resurrection in the light of the Holy Spirit.

(b) Also to be noted are the *different ways* of understanding the mystery of Christ that already appear in the New Testament books themselves. This is seen, however, when *an Old Testament mode of speaking* is employed, and when Scripture is said to be *fulfilled* in Jesus, the savior of the world. For the fulfilment of Scripture presupposes a certain *amplification of meaning,* whether it is a question of a meaning that the biblical texts originally bore, or of a meaning that Jews, rereading these texts, were attributing to them in the time of Jesus. Indeed, such an amplification of meaning should scarcely be attributed to secondary[37] theological *speculation;* it has its origin in the *person* of Jesus himself, whose own characteristics it sets in a better light.

1.1.11.3. With such considerations (these) exegetes and theologians approach the question of *the individual personality of Jesus.*

(a) This individual personality was cultivated and formed[38] by a Jewish education, the positive values of which Jesus took fully to himself. But it was also endowed with a *quite singular consciousness of himself,*[39] as far as his relation to God was concerned as well as the mission he was to carry out for human beings. Some Gospel texts (e.g. Luke 2:40, 52) lead us to recognize a certain *growth*[40] in this consciousness.

(b) Nevertheless, (these) exegetes and theologians refuse to get involved in a "psychology" of Jesus, both because of critical problems in the texts and because of the danger of speculating (in some wrong way, either by excess or by defect).[41] They prefer a reverent circumspection before the mystery of his personality. Jesus took no pains to define it precisely, even though through his sayings or his deeds he did allow one to catch a mere glimpse of the secrets of his intimate life (H. Schürmann). Various Christologies in the New Testament, as well as the definitions of councils—in which are repeated, in an "auxiliary language,"

---

[36]L has *humanitatis,* which is missing in F.
[37]L: *secundariae*; F: *simple.*
[38]F has only one verb, *a été façonnée.*
[39]L: *conscientia sui ipsius plane singulari*; F: *conscience de soi originale.*
[40]L: *progressum*; F: *développement.*
[41]F: *en raison du danger des spéculations abusives, qu'elles soient majorantes ou minimisantes.*

things already contained in Scripture—have indicated the *route* along which theological[42] speculation can proceed, without exactly demasking the mystery itself.

1.1.11.4. In their studies of Jesus Christ, (these) exegetes and theologians also agree that *Christology should in no way be separated from soteriology.* The Word of God was made flesh (Jn 1:14) to play the role of mediator between God and human beings. If he could be a human being "fully free" and "a man for others," that was so because this freedom and this gift of himself flowed forth from a source none other than the intimate union of himself with God, since he was able to turn to God as Father in a special and quite unique sense. Questions, then, about the knowledge and pre-existence of Christ can in no way be avoided; but each of them pertains to a later stage of Christology.

Chap. 2—The Risks and Limits of These Different Methodologies

Each of the approaches mentioned above has its strong points, is based on biblical texts, and also possesses advantages and stimulative qualities. But a number of the approaches, if used alone, run the risk of not explaining fully the biblical message or even of proposing a watered-down picture of Jesus Christ.[43]

1.2.1. *The approach of Classical Theology* encounters two hazards:

1.2.1.1. The formulation of doctrine about Christ *depends* more on *the language of theologians of the patristic period and the Middle Ages* than on the language of the New Testament itself, as if this ultimate source of the revelation (about him) were less accurate and less suited to setting forth a doctrine in well-defined terms.[44]

1.2.1.2. Recourse to the New Testament, if it is had with the sole concern of defending or establishing the so-called "traditional" doctrine in its "classical" formulation, runs the risk of *not being open,* as it ought to be, to *certain critical questions* that cannot be avoided in the exeget-

---

[42]L has *theologica,* which F omits.

[43]F adds a sentence: It is necessary then to judge precisely the limitations of several of them.

[44]F: as if this ultimate source of the revelation, in itself, were too imprecise to furnish the doctrine with a well-defined formulation.

ical area. For instance, it can happen that the historical character[45] of the texts is too easily admitted when in certain Gospel episodes it is a question of all the minute details. These might rather have had a theological purpose according to a literary convention of that time. Or the word-for-word authenticity of certain sayings attributed to Jesus in the Gospels (is again too easily admitted), even though they are recounted in diverse ways in different books.[46] Hence, a number of questions may be disregarded which are rightly discussed in our day. So it can happen that doctrinal propositions are made to rest on critical conclusions that are too "conservative," when in reality they are controversial.[47]

1.2.2. The attempt at theological speculation that proceeds from a *critique of the language employed by theologians and councils* is basically correct. But lest the testimony of Sacred Scripture be distorted, this critique must be tempered by two conditions.[48]

1.2.2.1. The "auxiliary" languages employed in the Church in the course of centuries do not enjoy the same authority, as far as faith is concerned, as the "referential language" of the inspired authors, especially (that) of the New Testament with its mode of expression rooted in the Prior (Testament). That *"the absolute value of the revelation"[49] may be grasped through the medium of some relative language,* even given the continuity between *the basic experience of* the apostolic Church and the subsequent *experience of the Church,* distinctions and analyses necessary for research[50] cannot be made if the express affirmations of Scripture are done away with.

1.2.2.2. In this matter the risk is that an absolute value be ascribed to modes of thinking and speaking that are proper to our age, with the result that the understanding of Christ which flows from the Gospels can be called in question. This would certainly be the case if New Testament

---

[45]L has *indoles textuum plane historica,* where the adverb *plane* is scarcely intelligible; F has rather: the historicity of all the details in certain Gospel episodes.

[46]F: in these Gospels.

[47]L: *in conclusionibus criticis nimis "conservativis," quae reapse in controversia versantur;* but F: critical solutions of a "conservative" type, which are disputed.

[48]F: two conditions are essential.

[49]L: *absolutum pondus revelationis;* F: *l'Absolu de la révélation.*

[50]L: *ad investigandum,* which is missing in F; the latter reads: the necessary distinctions and analyses cannot sacrifice the formal affirmations of Scripture.

texts were to be subjected to a selective process or an interpretation that various philosophical systems *would call for*. But a Christology cannot be solidly worked out unless the equilibrium be preserved that flows from Sacred Scripture taken as a whole and from the various modes of speaking which it employs.[51]

1.2.3. *Historical investigations* are of great importance for the understanding of people and events of bygone days, as is clear to everyone, and they are certainly also to be used with regard to Jesus of Nazareth. Obviously, one cannot disregard what historical investigation has uncovered about the circumstances of times and places in which the testimonies (about him) have been received and passed on (cf. 1.1.3 above).

1.2.3.1. Nevertheless, the simple analysis of texts does not suffice. For those texts were composed and received in a community of human beings that lived not on abstract ideas but on faith. This faith has its origin and progressive growth in Jesus' resurrection; it was an event of salvation introduced among people who already shared the religious experience of diverse Jewish communities.[52]

1.2.3.2. Since a great difference is noted between the faith of Jewish communities and the faith of the Christian Church, one could easily become oblivious of the historical continuity between the primitive faith of the apostles based on "the law of Moses, the Prophets, and the Psalms" (Lk 24:44) and the faith which they themselves acquired from their relations with the risen Christ. Yet this continuity is equally a historical fact. There was continuity in their religious recognition of the God of Abraham and of Moses both before and after the Easter event. They lived with "the historical Jesus" before they lived with "the Christ of faith." Hence, no matter what may be the subjective inclinations of today's experts, it is incumbent on all to investigate that *profound unity* that the Christology of the New Testament manifests as intimately bound up in its own development.

---

[51]L is garbled here: *quod effluit e Sacra Scriptura in toto apprehensa variis e que loquendi modis quibus utitur*. F: *qui résulte de l'ensemble de l'Ecriture et en assumant la variété des langages qu'elle utilise*.

[52]F: which did not live on abstract ideas, but on a nascent faith that gradually deepened in the resurrection of Jesus, an event of salvation inserted into the experience of diverse Jewish communities.

1.2.4. Though the aid that comes from the *comparative study of religion* is needed in any inquiry into the origins of the Christian religion, the use of it runs two risks.

1.2.4.1. It can be vitiated by a *preconceived view*: that the religion of Christ has to be explained, as in analogous cases, by a *fusion* or *syncretism* of elements pre-existent in the social milieu in which this religion arose, viz. some from Judaism, some from contemporary ethnic religions:[53] the religion of Christ would have sprung from the joining of a certain group of believers of Jewish background with a Hellenistic social milieu, from which it had to pick up a number of elements. But as early as the third century B.C. *Judaism had already confronted the problems of Hellenization,* either by rejecting elements contrary to its own tradition or by assimilating good elements with which it could be enriched. When, however, it passed on to subsequent ages the Sacred Scriptures translated into Greek, it already manifested the success of its own "inculturation." Early Christianity, which inherited these translated Scriptures, followed along the same path.

1.2.4.2. There is also the risk of ascribing to primitive Christian communities a creative force deprived of all internal check, as if individual churches were without roots[54] or a solid tradition. Some historians have gone so far as to regard Christ as nothing more than "a myth" devoid of all historicity. Such a view, paradoxical as it is, is usually avoided; but not a few historians who are nonbelievers maintain that Christian communities emerging from Hellenism transformed the "savior" of the Jewish tradition into the chief "hero" of a "religion of salvation," scarcely different from the cults of the *mystery religions.* The comparative study of religions, however, does not require such an evolutionistic principle that would be the foundation for such an interpretation. It tries to uncover "the constant laws"[55] in the history of religions, but it does not level out religious beliefs so as to deform them. As in the study of other religions, so too in the study of the Christian religion, the task of such investigation is to discover the *specific character of the religion of Christ,* linked to the newness of the gospel. Thus,

---

[53]F: *des paganismes contemporains.*
[54]L: *radicibus*; F: *encadrement.*
[55]F: the constants.

by the skew of phenomenology, it too can open a way to Christology itself.

1.2.5. *The diligent study of Judaism* is of utmost importance for the correct understanding of the person of Jesus, as well as of the early Church and its specific[56] faith.

1.2.5.1. If to understand Jesus studies are conducted *only* along these lines, there is always the danger of mutilating his personality, precisely at the moment when stress is being put by such studies on his Jewish background and character. Would he be only one of many teachers, even if the most faithful of all to the tradition of the Law and the Prophets? Or a prophet, a victim of a disastrous mistake? Or a wonder-worker like others whose memory has been preserved in monuments of Jewish literature? Or even a political instigator finally put to death by Roman authorities in collusion with the chief priests, who did not understand him?

1.2.5.2. It is true that the disputes in which Jesus was involved with groups of Pharisees espousing stricter discipline[57] do not seem to differ from controversies among brothers who share the same heritage. But the vitality later on[58] of the movement that started with him clearly shows that the chief cause of that disagreement was much more profound, even though we admit that the Gospel accounts could have described more harshly than was right the original state of affairs.[59] For this disagreement had as its object a new way of understanding one's relation to God and "the fulfilment of Scripture," which Jesus had brought to the people of his time through the gospel of the kingdom.[60] An accurate study of Jesus' Jewish character cannot pass over this aspect of him.

1.2.6. As for the approach to Jesus Christ from the idea of so-called *salvation history,* one has to agree that it has introduced important advantages into the study, even if the expression *Heilsgeschichte* be too

---

[56]L: *peculiaris*: F: *originale*.

[57]F: It is correct that the tensions that set Jesus is opposition to the pietist current of Pharisees resemble the controversies. . . .

[58]F adds: after his rejection by the religious leaders of his nation.

[59]F: even if one admits that in this regard the Gospel accounts could have hardened the original situation.

[60]F adds: of God.

vague. The questions raised by this approach vary with the different proponents who espouse it.

1.2.6.1. In modern languages derived from Latin as well as in English, the word "history" does not have the same meaning when it is a question of Jesus as a "historical" person and of "salvation history." German makes a distinction between *Historie* and *Geschichte*; but the terminology to be used really poses a difficult question. For the historical understanding of Jesus is based on empirical facts or on experience, access to which is gained by the study of documents.[61] But so-called "salvation history" is not so based. It embraces a common experience, but it presupposes a certain *understanding* to which one has access only by the intelligence that comes with faith. This distinction must always be kept in mind so that Christology may be put in a true and proper perspective. This suggests that in both the historian and the theologian there must be an open-mindedness toward a lively faith[62] and toward the "decision of faith," by which access to it is gained.

1.2.6.2. This consideration must be applied in a special way to *the resurrection of Christ,* which by its very nature cannot be proved in an empirical way. For by it Jesus is introduced into "the world to come." This can, indeed, be deduced as a reality from the appearances of Christ in glory to certain preordained witnesses,[63] and it is corroborated by the fact that Jesus' tomb was found open and empty. But one may not simplify this question excessively, as if any historian, making use only of scientific investigation, could prove it with certainty as a fact accessible to any observer whatsoever. In this matter there is also needed "the decision of faith," or better "an open heart," so that the mind may be moved to assent.[64]

1.2.6.3. As for the titles of Christ, it is not sufficient to distinguish between those titles that Jesus used of himself during his earthly life and those that were given to him by theologians of the apostolic age. It is more important to make the distinction between *functional titles,* by

---

[61]F: The history of Jesus belongs, in fact, to the *empirical domain* accessible through the study of documents.

[62]F: to the life of faith.

[63]F: to privileged witnesses.

[64]F: here once again, the "decision of faith," or better, the "openness of heart," controls the position taken.

which the roles of Christ are defined in his salvific activity on behalf of humanity, and *relational titles,* which pertain to his relation to God, of whom he is both the Word and the Son. In the treatment of this question, Jesus' *habits, deeds, and conduct* are to be examined no less than the titles, since they reveal what is most profound about a person.

1.2.6.4. That *salvation history is tending toward eschatology* and that a hope springs from this (tendency) brings with it consequences important for Christian "praxis" in human societies. But the word "eschatology" is in itself ambiguous. Are "the last times" to be regarded as beyond historical experience? Did Jesus announce the end of "this world" before the generation of his own time would pass away? Or did he thus introduce a new way of considering the conditions in which the course of human history would run? Was it not rather a question of the last stage of the *oikonomia* of salvation, inaugurated by the message of the gospel of the kingdom, but not yet consummated, which extends through the entire span of church history? A Christology true to its colors ought to explain all questions of this sort.

1.2.7. The risk run by the *anthropological approaches* to Christology, which embrace a whole gamut of different modes of reflection, is noted in their tendency to play down certain components that make up a human person in his existence and history. Hence a Christology that is defective can emerge in this way.

1.2.7.1. With regard to *the human phenomenon,* has its *religious aspect* been sufficiently studied in its historical development so that the person of Jesus and the founding of the Church are precisely situated in their Jewish milieu within the course of universal evolution? Does the optimistic interpretation of this evolution, aimed at the "Omega point," allow sufficiently for *questions about evil* and for the redemptive activity of the death of Jesus, even if account is otherwise taken of the crises that human evolution is to overcome? Studies about the person of Jesus and about the Christologies of the New Testament will supply the complements needed in this matter.

1.2.7.2. Speculative attempts dealing with *the philosophical analysis of human existence* run the risk of being rejected by those who do not grant the philosophical premises involved. Certainly, the biblical data (regarding Jesus Christ) are not disregarded (in this approach); but they ought often to be scrutinized anew in order that the demands of biblical criticism[65] and the multiplicity of the New Testament Christologies be better met. Only in this way can a philosophical anthropology be rightly applied, on the one hand, to the personal existence of Jesus in this world, and, on the other, to the role that the glorified Christ plays in Christian existence.

1.2.7.3. It is legitimate, indeed, to begin *a historical investigation about Jesus considering him as a true human being,* but that involves many things:[66] his life as a Jew; his way of acting and his preaching; the awareness that he had of himself and the way he proposed his mission; the preview he had of his death and the meaning that he could have given to it; the origin of faith in his resurrection and the ways of interpreting his death in the early Church; the progressive working out of a Christology and a soteriology in the New Testament. But the risk is that *doctrinal elements amassed in this way depend too much on the critical hypotheses* employed at the outset to achieve this end. If as a result of this methodology only those hypotheses are admitted that are as restrictive as possible, then a Christology emerges that is lacunary. That is especially noticed when texts regarded as "older" are taken as the only trustworthy ones, whereas the more recent texts are written off as speculations born of a later period[67] that have completely[68] changed the "original" data coming from the "the historical Jesus." Were not these (later) texts[69] rather aimed at making *more explicit,* thanks to new meditation on the Prior Testament and a deeper reflection upon Jesus' words and deeds, *a faith-understanding* of Christ—such as was present from the beginning, as it were, in a kernel and implicitly? The risk is that the role played by the Prior Testament, the authority of which neither Jesus nor his disciples ever called in question, is too much disregarded in this matter. The result is that the very interpretation of the New Testament may turn out to be erroneous.

1.2.7.4. Legitimate, indeed, is the attempt *to establish continuity between Jesus' experience and that of Christians.* But then it must also be established, without reliance on hypotheses that are too minimal, how

---

[65]F omits "biblical."
[66]The last clause is missing in F.
[67]F: secondary speculations.
[68]F: substantially.
[69]F adds: *à leur époque.*

and in what sense Jesus, "the eschatological prophet," came to be acknowledged in faith as the Son of God; how the inchoative faith and hope of his disciples could come to be transformed into a firm certitude about his triumph over death; how among the conflicts that affected the churches of the apostolic period, one was able finally to come to recognize the *true "praxis"* that Christ desired—that which was the basis of the authentic "sequel of Jesus"; how, finally, the different interpretations of his person and mission as mediator of God and human beings, which are found in the New Testament, could at length be considered as presenting the *true* picture of Jesus, as he really was, and of the revelation that took place in him and through him. Only on such conditions will ambiguity be avoided in proposing a Christology.

1.2.8. *The approach (to Christology) based on an existential analysis.* In constantly demanding of believers that they bear themselves before God according to the example of obedience given by Jesus himself, (this approach) brings to light the close connection joining exegesis, theological study, and living faith. By an accurate critical analysis of the texts, this method often discovers the function played by the texts in the Christian communities for which they were composed—and consequently their function too in the Church of today. Nevertheless, many exegetes and theologians, of differing confessional backgrounds, have pointed out the limits and the deficiencies of this approach.

1.2.8.1. *Those who espouse a radical critique* have limited the scope of their Gospel studies to a very tiny nucleus, the more so because they consider the knowledge of Jesus as a historical personage to be of minimal importance for faith. And so *Jesus would no longer really be at the origin of Christology.* Christology would have rather taken its start from the Easter kerygma, not from the existence of Jesus, a Jew who in himself fulfilled the law (= *Torah*) under which he lived. But if this law has as its only function to show by its own collapse that human beings cannot save themselves, does not the entire theology of the Prior Testament also disappear into thin air?

1.2.8.2. *The symbolic language* used in the New Testament to pass on the Easter kerygma, in order to declare who Christ is and in what his role consists, is restricted to the limits of "mythological" language. As a result, *the relation between the two Testaments is reduced to the extreme.* Finally, does not the "existential" (or "existentialist") interpretation proposed for the understanding of "mythological" language run the risk of reducing Christology to an *anthropology*?[70]

1.2.8.3. If Christ's resurrection and exaltation are to be considered only as mythological transformations of the Easter message, it is not understandable how Christian faith could have been born of the cross. Again, if Jesus is not the Son of God in a unique sense, it is scarcely evident why God has addressed His "last word" to us in him through the medium of the cross. Finally, if, to get around the rationalistic conception of "proofs" that establish the faith, the "signs" on which it is based are also suppressed, is not this, in effect, an invitation to fideism?

1.2.8.4. To the extent that this approach to Jesus would consist exclusively in a *decision of faith,* would not the *social aspects of human existence* be excluded? Again, in this way a certain "morality of love," vaguely defined, would be radically opposed to a "morality of law" that should include the positive demands of justice. For all these reasons the disciples of R. Bultmann have undertaken to restore Jesus *to the origins of Christology,* without rejecting the global aim of his interpretation based on an "existential" analysis.

1.2.9. Proponents of *liberation theology* rightly recall that the salvation brought by Christ is not solely "spiritual," i.e. wholly dissociated from affairs of this world.[71] It is intended to free human beings, by God's grace indeed, from every tyranny oppressing them in their present situation. However, from such a general principle risky consequences can be drawn, especially if the doctrine of the redemption is not clearly joined to a system of ethics that is fully consonant with the precepts of the New Testament.

1.2.9.1. Though some Marxists indirectly refer to Jesus' gospel to find in it the ideal form of social life based on brotherly relations, they do not abandon their *method of analysis of social facts*[72] from an economic and political point of view. This method is tied to a *philosophical anthropology,* the theoretic basis of which includes atheism. This method of investigation and the "praxis" associated with it, when adopted uncritically, so that the God of the Bible becomes the artisan of

---

[70]F: does it not risk ending logically in an *anthropological* reduction of Christology?
[71]For the last phrase F merely has: disembodied (*désincarné*).
[72]F: But that leaves intact their method of analysis.

the "liberation" so conceived, runs the risk of falsifying the very nature of God, the correct interpretation of Christ, and in the long run even the understanding and comprehension of humanity itself.

1.2.9.2. Some "liberation theologians" firmly maintain that "the Christ of faith" has to be retained as the ultimate principle of hope. Yet, in reality, only the "praxis" of the "Jesus of history" is actually considered, portrayed even more or less arbitrarily with a "mode of reading" of the text that partly falsifies it. Hence, "the Christ of faith" is considered as a mere "ideological" interpretation, or even a "mythologization" of his historical personage. Moreover, since the idea of "power" in the Christian communities, subjected as they were at that time to the Roman empire and its local governors, is given no accurate analysis, that idea itself runs the serious risk of being interpreted with Marxist nuances.

1.2.9.3. Consequently, the activity of Christ the liberator at work through the Holy Spirit in the Church is no longer considered. Jesus is no more than a "model" of the past. His "praxis" is to be promoted by other means better suited to our times and capable of greater results. In this way Christology runs the risk of being completely *reduced to anthropology*.

1.2.10. *Studies in speculative theology about Christ* take as a principle, and not without reason, the refusal *to depend on critical hypotheses* that are always subject to revision. There is, however, in this approach the danger that, because of an excessive concern to make a synthesis, *the variety of New Testament Christologies* be obscured, when in reality that variety is to be greatly esteemed. Or even that the elements in *the Prior Testament that are preparatory* be dismissed or so belittled that the New Testament would be deprived of its roots. It is desirable that exegetical studies find a more precise and well-defined place in the study of revelation, which from the beginning and through the whole course of its development has been tending toward its ultimate goal in the totality of the mystery of Christ. Herein lies a certain divine "pedagogy," in a sense different from that of Paul (Gal 3:24), that is leading humanity to Christ.

1.2.11. All attempts to unite a *Christology "from below" with a Christology "from above"* are on the right track. However, they leave in suspense certain questions that call for an answer.

1.2.11.1. In the area of exegetical studies many problems remain to be resolved, in particular *critical questions* about the Gospels: the way the sayings of Jesus have come to be formulated in them; the more or less "historical" character (in the strict sense) of the narratives that concern Jesus;[73] the date and authorship of individual books; the modes and stages of their composition; and the development of Christological doctrine. This area of studies lies open to investigation; it is not only legitimate but even necessary and capable of bearing fruit for systematic Christology itself.

1.2.11.2. In order to comprehend the great and *unique importance that Christ has in the course of world history,* one cannot dispense with a study of the place of the Bible in the development of various cultures. Because these sacred books enter the history of these cultures at a relatively[74] late date, one must not disregard the way certain elements of these cultures were taken up into the books, to be used in the service of revelation. *The Jewish character* of Jesus, inserted into various cultures, is somehow the bearer of *his total humanity.* This approach to Jesus, spurred on especially by archeological and ethnological discoveries of the last two centuries, has scarcely been tapped. But in order to understand how Jesus is the savior of *all* human beings of *all* ages, one has to consider his pre-existence, recognizing him as the Wisdom of God and the Word of God (cf. the Johannine Prologue), as well as the author and exemplar of creation and the powerful governor of the whole course of human history.

1.2.11.3. Moreover, to understand how *the glorified Christ continues to act effectively in this world,*[75] more accurate studies of Scripture have to be undertaken concerning the relations between the Church, which is his body guided by the Holy Spirit, and the societies in which it develops. Given such a consideration, *ecclesiology* becomes *an essential aspect of Christology,* and precisely at the moment when it is confronted by the studies of sociologists.

---

[73]L: *indoles plus minusque "historica" stricto sensu narrationum quae ad Eum attinent;* F: *l'historicité plus ou moins dense des récits qui le concernent.*

[74]L: *sero;* F: *à une date relativement tardive.*

[75]L: *quomodo Christus glorificatus efficaciter operans maneat in hoc mundo;* F: *comment le Christ glorifié continue d'agir efficacement dans ce monde-ci.*

Chap. 3—How Are Such Risks, Limitations, or Ambiguities To Be Avoided?

The approaches mentioned above show that it would not be sufficient, in order that remedies be found for all such risks, to set forth a few trenchant formulas proposing the definitive "truth" or even to work out systematic treatises that would handle all these problems and solve them right off.

1.3.1. *Solidarity in faith* with the whole ecclesiastical tradition bids biblical scholars[76] to have constant recourse to *the basic tradition* of apostolic times (understood broadly to embrace the whole New Testament). This solidarity, however, in no way excuses one from engaging in studies *of the Bible as a whole*: of the place that it had in Israel, and of the new branch grafted into it through Jesus Christ with the writings of the New Testament up to the closing off of the "canon," i.e. the *norm* for Christian faith and life.[77] With regard to this last point, though a fundamental disagreement exists between Jews and Christians, nevertheless the principle of canonicity is firmly established for both of them.

1.3.2. The literary development of the Bible itself is in a way a reflection of that gift of God that has brought his revelation and salvation to human beings. For Christians the apex of this gift is the Son of God, true man "born of the Virgin Mary." The unity in the Scriptures is thus seen in the promises received by the patriarchs, expanded through the prophets, then through the expectation of God's kingdom and of a Messiah; but these promises and this expectation have found fulfilment in Jesus, the Messiah and Son of God. The use of Scripture in Christology is governed, then, by *the principle of totality,* which the Fathers and the medieval theologians well recalled,[78] even though they were reading and interpreting the biblical texts according to methods suited to the culture of their own times. Other, indeed, are the methods that the culture of our age furnishes; but the way to make use of them and their goal remain the same.[79]

---

[76]F: tells the theologian.

[77]F: up to the closing of the "canonical" list, i.e. normative for faith and practical life.

[78]F: which neither the Fathers nor the medieval theologians ever neglected.

[79]F: but the orientation according to which one must use them remains the same.

1.3.3. That readers who are believers may discover this *integral Christology* in the Scriptures, it is a desideratum that *biblical studies* be conducted with the aid of the exegetical methods of our age and that they become more advanced in research and investigation than they are at present. Indeed, many problems still remain obscure about the composition process of the sacred writings that finally emerged from their inspired authors. As a result, those who would dispense with the study of problems of this sort would be approaching Scripture only in a superficial way; wrongly judging that their way of reading Scripture is "theological," they would be setting off on a deceptive route. Solutions that are too easy[80] can in no way provide the solid basis needed for studies in biblical theology, even when engaged in with full faith. But the Pontifical Biblical Commission judges that, if one prescinds from details of minor importance, such studies have made sufficient progress that *any believer can find in their results a solid basis for his/her study about Jesus Christ.*

The following treatment, divided into two chapters, takes up these questions: 1. Promises and expectation of salvation and of a savior in the Prior Testament; 2. Fulfilment of these promises and expectation in the person of Jesus of Nazareth.

PART II
THE GLOBAL TESTIMONY OF
SACRED SCRIPTURE ABOUT CHRIST

Chap. 1—God's Salvific Deeds and the Messianic Hope in Israel

Jesus and the primitive Christian community clearly acknowledged the divine authority of the Scriptures that we call the Prior or the Old Testament. Indeed, as its sacred writers have borne witness, Israel came to believe that its God had willed its salvation and that He was also aware of its paths. This primary experience of the relations between God and His people stands, then, on a solid basis, and its importance rightly demands that it be properly assessed.

---

[80]F: oversimplified (*simplistes*).

In these writings, then, three items are to be considered that Christians will find to have been completely fulfilled in Christ Jesus: (a) *the knowledge of the true God,* who is distinct from all other gods and the basis of Israel's hope; (b) the experience of God's *salvific will*[81] that Israel enjoyed in the course of its history amid other peoples; (c) the different *forms of mediation* by which the observance of the covenant and the communing of God and humanity were continually promoted. It is not a question here of sketching various stages of the divine revelation made to Israel, but rather of recalling the principal witnesses in this "Prior Testament," to which the Christian community listened and which it understood in the light of Christ who had already come.

2.1.1. GOD AND THE REVELATION OF HIM IN THE PRIOR TESTAMENT

2.1.1.1. All peoples of the ancient Near East seeking for God were, "as it were, groping for him" (Acts 17:27). According to the Book of Wisdom, they went astray in their quest because, captivated by the beauty of things, they considered the powers of this world to be gods and paid no attention to how much more beautiful was the One who had fashioned them (13:3). Yet God manifested Himself to Israel as One seeking out human beings: He calls Abraham (Gen 12:1–3) and grants him descendants that will become His own people among all the peoples of the earth (Exod 19:5–6; Deut 7:6), and indeed out of sheer favor (Deut 7:8). In Abraham and his posterity the nations of the earth will receive their blessing (Gen 12:3; 22:18; 26:4). In this God alone they will find salvation (Isa 45:22–25), and on Him alone they are to base their hope (Isa 51:4–5).

2.1.1.2. God, *the creator* of the universe (Gen 1:1–2:4), manifests himself to Israel especially as the *Lord* and *Moderator*[82] of history (Amos 1:3–2:16; Isa 10:5 ff.). He is "the First and the Last," and besides Him there is no other god who can act as He does (Isa 44:6; 45:5–6). There is no God but in Israel (Isa 45:14), and He is the only one (Isa 45:5). In a special sense He manifests Himself to human beings as *king.* Though He has already revealed this kingly authority by His power in

---

[81]F uses this phrase in the plural, *des volontés de salut.*
[82]F: Lord and Master.

creation (Ps 93:1–2; 95:3–5), He displays it still more in caring for the fortunes of Israel (Exod 15:18; Isa 52:7) and for His kingdom yet to come (Psalm 98). This kingly authority finds its central focus in the worship that is paid to God in the city of Jerusalem (Isa 6:1–5; Psalm 122). After Israel on its own chose masters for itself (1 Sam 8:1–9) and finally experienced the heavy yoke of such kings (1 Sam 8:10–20), it then found in its God the good shepherd (Psalm 23; Ezekiel 34), for he is ever "faithful . . . just and upright" (Deut 32:4), "merciful and clement . . . patient and rich in kindness and fidelity" (Exod 34:6).

God, then, as one close to human beings, constitutes, as it were, the very substance[83] of Israel's faith. His name, expressed by the tetragram YHWH, is an acknowledgment of this faith (cf. Exod 3:12–15), and it at once defines the form of the relation into which He wants to enter with His people, as He summons them to fidelity.

2.1.2. GOD AND HUMANITY: PROMISES AND COVENANT

2.1.2.1. By His own unswerving will (Jer 31:35–37), made manifest in an oath sworn "by Himself" (Gen 22:16–18), this God has entered into a pact with human beings fashioned into a people.[84] He set over this people leaders whom He bade carry out His designs: Abraham (Gen 18:19), Moses (Exod 3:7–15), the "judges" (Judg 2:16–18), and kings (2 Sam 7:8–16). Through their activity God was going to free His people from every bondage or foreign domination (Exod 3:8; Josh 24:10; 2 Sam 7:9–11), give them the promised land (Gen 15:18; 22:17; Josh 24:8–13; 2 Sam 7:10), and finally bring about deliverance (Exod 15:2; Judg 2:16–18). Through their activity God was likewise going to pass on to this people His commandments and laws (Gen 18:19; Exod 15:25; 21:1; Deut 5:1; 12:1; Josh 24:25–27; 1 Kgs 2:3). The observance of these commandments and laws was to be the special way in which Israel would acknowledge its faith in God, thus expressing respect for the person and property of its neighbors (Exod 20:3–17; Deut 5:6–21; Exod 21:2 ff.; Lev 19). The connection between this gift of the land and obedience to the law is expressed in Scripture under the juridical notion of "cove-

---

[83]F: constitutes the very heart of Israel's faith.
[84]F: human beings fashioned as one people.

nant'' (*bĕrît*). By it new bonds are set that God decides to establish between Himself and human beings.

Clearly this people and its leaders freely submit themselves to this covenant (Exod 24:3–8; Deut 29:9–14; Josh 24:14–24). They were, however, always being seduced by temptation to worship gods other than YHWH (Exod 32:1–6; Num 25:1–18; Judg 2:11–13), to oppress their neighbors with every form of injustice (Amos 2:6–8; Hos 4:1–2; Isa 1:22–23; Jer 5:1 ff.), and so to break that ''covenant'' made with God (Deut 31:16, 20; Jer 11:10; 32:32; Ezek 44:7). Some of their kings were especially notorious in the practice of such injustice (Jer 22:13–17) and in breaking the covenant (Ezek 17:11–21). Nevertheless, God's fidelity would at length overcome the infidelity of human beings (Hos 2:20–22), by concluding a new covenant with them (Jer 31:31–34), a covenant that would be everlasting and unbreakable (Jer 32:40; Ezek 37:26–27). This covenant, indeed, would be extended not only to Abraham's posterity marked by the sign of circumcision (Gen 17:9–13), but to all human beings by the sign of the rainbow in the sky (Gen 9:12–17; cf. Isa 25:6; 66:18).

2.1.2.2. The prophets denounced the scandal caused by the manifold violation[85] of this covenant, which they witnessed: that was the reason why the people chosen by God were condemned (2 Kgs 17:7–23). Nevertheless, the prophets too became the main witnesses of God's fidelity, which was to surpass all human infidelities. For this same God would radically transform the human heart, granting it the ability to satisfy its obligations through obedience to the law (Jer 31:33–34; Ezek 36:26–28). Though the covenant was being broken so often by Israel,[86] the prophets never lost hope that God would one day bring deliverance to (His) people because of His boundless love and leniency (Amos 7:1–6; Hos 11:1–9; Jer 31:1–9)—and this even when (their) history was at its saddest (Ezek 37:1–4).

For in David God had fulfilled His earlier promises to make out of many tribes Israel, a free people in its own land (2 Sam 7:9–11). Though David's successors scarcely followed in his footsteps, the prophets looked forward to *that king* who, as David had done (2 Sam 8:15), *would*

---

[85]F: If the prophets have been scandalized witnesses of this breach of the covenant in all its forms.

[86]F: Despite, then, the repeated breaches of the covenant on Israel's part.

administer equity and justice, especially to the poorest and the lowliest in the realm (Isa 9:5–6; Jer 23:5–6; 33:15–16). Such a king would manifest God's "zeal" toward His people (Isa 9:6) and would assure the peace promised from the beginning (Amos 9:11–12; Ezek 34:23–31; 37:24–27).

The prophets also announced in advance that the city of Jerusalem, (once) purified, would also be restored, (as the place) where God would dwell in His temple. To it would be given certain symbolic names, e.g. "City of Righteousness" (Isa 1:26), "The Lord Is Our Righteousness" (Jer 33:16), "The Lord Is There" (Ezek 48:35); and its walls would be called "Salvation," its gates "Praise" (Isa 60:18). All nations, already related to the everlasting covenant of David (Isa 55:3–5), would be called to share in the salvation of the God of Israel in the holy restored city (Isa 62:10–12), because from Zion would go forth law and righteousness, to be extended to the ends of the earth (Isa 2:1–5; Mic 4:1–4); in YHWH alone would they find salvation (Isa 51:4–8).

2.1.3. VARIOUS WAYS OF MEDIATING SALVATION

2.1.3.1. It is indeed God Himself who saves His people and the whole human race; but to do this He makes use of different forms of mediation.

(a) *The king* occupies a special place in this coming of salvation. In adopting the king as a son (2 Sam 7:14; Ps 2:7; 110:3 LXX; 89:27–28), God confers on him the power to conquer his people's enemies (2 Sam 7:9–11; Ps 2:8–9; 110:1 ff.; 89:23–24). With this power the judges had earlier been graced as saviors (Judg 2:16). Endowed with divine wisdom (1 Kgs 3:4–15, 28), the king was to be faithful to the God of the covenant (1 Kgs 11:11; 2 Kgs 22:2) and see to it that equity and justice would be preserved throughout his realm, especially toward the poor, the widows, and the orphans (Isa 11:3–5; Jer 22:15–16; Ps 72:1–4, 12–14). Rightly, the Book of Deuteronomy insists on the king's obligation to carry out all his covenantal duties (Deut 17:16–20). Moreover, only if the king is faithful in preserving justice will he insure the peace and freedom of his people (Ps 72:7–11; Jer 23:6; Isa 11:5–9). If, however, as (often) happened, the king is found faithless in covenantal obligations, he will drag the people with him into disaster[87] (Jer 21:12; 22:13–19). The nations themselves are everywhere invited to share in the blessings of this gift given to humanity by God (Ps 72:17).

(b) Though kings performed priestly functions (2 Sam 6:13, 17–18; 1 Kgs 8:63 ff.; etc.), such functions were properly carried out by the levitical *priest* (Deut 18:1–8). Yet that priestly function is strikingly defined by its relation to the law (Jer 18:18): the priest is the guardian of the law (Hos 4:6; Deut 31:9); he teaches (Mal 2:6–7) the various commandments that make it up (Deut 33:10). In his cultic function he sanctifies himself as well as the whole Israelite community so that the offering of a sacrifice acceptable to God may be possible (Deut 33:10). But since divine[88] worship used to celebrate past events of salvation (Ps 132; 136 . . .) and recall Israel's obligations toward God (Isa 1:10–20; Hos 8:11–13; Amos 5:21–25; Mic 6:6–8), priestly worship, according to the unambiguous testimony of the prophets, only achieves its end to the degree that each priest performs his role as a minister of the law (Hos 4:6–10).

(c) *The prophet* performed a function of great importance in Israel in its experience of salvation throughout its history.[89] Haunted by "the word of God" (Jer 18:18), a prophet is always present at the most serious crises of (this) history (Jer 1:10). The primary task imposed on him is to denounce the infidelities either of the people or (their) leaders, in political as well as in religious matters (1 Kgs 18). For the honor of his God, the prophet demands that respect be shown to human beings both in their persons and in their property, according to the commands of the Sinaitic covenant (1 Kgs 21; Amos 2:6–8; 5:7–13; Hos 4:1–2; Mic 3:1–4; Jer 7:9). Every transgression of the law[90] calls forth God's judgment on the sinful people, which the intercession even of the prophet himself cannot avert (Amos 7:7–9; 8:1–3). Only the sincere conversion of the unfaithful will bring it about that God will again manifest His salvation (Amos 5:4–6; Jer 4:1–2; Ezek 18:21–23; Joel 2:12–17). Yet since this sort of con-

---

[87]L: *secum trahet ruinam populi sui.*

[88]F omits the adjective "divine."

[89]F: The prophet played an important role in the experience that Israel had of salvation.

[90]F: The scorning of the law.

version is seen to be ephemeral and fragile (Hos 6:4), if not entirely impossible (Jer 13:23), only God can bring it about (Jer 31:18; Ezek 36:22). That is why the prophet can announce better times for the future, even when disasters are the most serious (Hos 2:20–23; Isa 46:8–13; Jer 31:31–34; Ezekiel 37). This sort of paedagogy prepares for the victory of divine love over the sinful condition in which humanity is mired (Hos 11:1–9; Isa 54:4–10).

It is the lot of *the sage,* the teacher of wisdom, to perceive the sense of this universe, which the Creator has entrusted to human beings (Sir 16:24–17:14), as at once the gift of God and the manifestation of His goodness (Gen 1:1–2:4; Psalm 8). The sage must also gather and rightly assess, in the light of revelation, the varied experiences of human beings, of persons who live in society and are obligated to pass on such experiences to coming generations, either as a goal to be aimed at and attained (Proverbs 1–7), or as a mystery to be respected (Prov 30:18–19). But it can happen that the sage may overrate his own counsels (Isa 5:21; 29:13–14) and, led on by them, may even do violence to the law of the Lord (Jer 8:8–9). Hence it is of great importance that the sage come to realize the limits of such wisdom so as to acquire for humanity happiness and prosperity (Qoh 1:12–2:26).

2.1.3.2. History itself has shown[91] that these *different forms of mediation proved inadequate* to establish for human beings an abiding mode of communing with God. After continued recurrence of setbacks, God stirred up in the conscience[92] of His people the hope of new mediators, through whose activity His kingdom would at length be permanently inaugurated.

(a) In comparison with bygone Davidic monarchs, the *King-Messiah* would be lowly; he would put an end to war and bring peace to all nations (Zech 9:9–10; cf. Ps 2:10–12). Though the definitive inauguration of this messianic kingdom would be the work of God Himself (Dan 2:44–45), it would be achieved through the activity[93] of His holy people (Dan 7:27), when "everlasting justice" and "the anointing of the Holy of Holies" (Dan 9:24) would take place.

(b) A *Servant of the Lord,* still enshrouded in deep mystery, would

---

[91]L: *res ipsae testatae sunt;* F: *l'histoire a montré.*
[92]F adds the adjective "religious."
[93]L: *opera*; F: *la médiation.*

seal a universal covenant, manifest to the whole world the unique and true Savior-God, and inaugurate an order decreed by God (Isa 42:1–4; 49:1–6). Sharing in the sufferings of his straying people, he would bear the weight of all (their) sins in order to bring the many to righteousness (Isa 52:13–53:12).

(c) Finally, when the times would be fulfilled, there would appear *the Son of Man* (then interpreted as the people, "the saints of the Most High," Dan 7:18), "coming before God with the clouds of heaven" (Dan 7:13–14), to receive eternal power over all peoples of the earth who would obey him (Dan 7:27).

2.1.3.3. To depict their faith in this activity of God in the world and human history, the people of Israel employed *certain figurative powers*[94] (which in pagan religions were even considered at times as deities, but which were subordinated to the God of Abraham), to express His creative and salvific presence.

(a) *The Spirit* as a force of God presided over the creation of all things and does not cease to renew them (Ps 104:29–30). It is especially at work in the course of history. As God's power, it makes human beings capable of accomplishing certain tasks. It is the Spirit that takes possession of the judges to set Israel free (Judg 3:10; 6:34; 11:29); that comes down upon king David (1 Sam 16:13) that he may bear the perfect image of a king (Isa 11:2)[95] and upon the Servant of the Lord (Isa 42:1–4)—to make all of them true mediators of God's kingdom in the world. It is the Spirit that gives prophets an understanding of their times (Ezek 2:1–7; Mic 3:8) and a hope of approaching salvation (Isa 61:1–3). In the end-time the same Spirit will create a new people that will rise from the dead (Ezek 37:1–14) to keep God's commands (Ezek 36:26–28). Finally, every human being will be inhabited by this Spirit that will open to him the gate of salvation (Joel 3:1–5).

(b) *The Word of God* has not only been given to human beings as a message (cf. Deut 4:13 and 10:4: the "ten words"), but it is also and in a special sense an active force that reveals everything. For God Himself by His word "spoke, and it was made" (Ps 33:6–9; cf. Gen 1:3 ff.). Creation was the work of His Word as well as of (His) Spirit (Ps 33:6). God's words, put into the mouths of prophets (Jer 1:9), become for them

---

[94]L: *quarundam potestatum figuris;* F: *figures de certaines puissances.*
[95]F: upon the ideal king (Isa 11:2).

at times a joy (Jer 15:16) and at times a fire (burning) in their bones (Jer 20:9, cf. 23:29). Finally, the Word, as also the Spirit, gradually assumes personal traits: it settles in the mouth and in the heart of Israel (Deut 30:14); "it stands firm forever in heaven" (Ps 119:89); it is sent forth to fulfil tasks entrusted to it (Wis 18:15–16) and never returns ineffective (Isa 55:11). The rabbinic tradition will insist greatly on this figure: then the word of God (*Memra*) will make manifest the activity of God Himself in His relations with the world.

(c) *Wisdom,* in the Book of Proverbs, is no longer only an attribute proper to kings or an art whereby one succeeds in life; it also appears as divine creative Wisdom (Prov 3:19–20; cf. 8:22 ff.). By it kings are enabled to govern (8:15–16); it invites humans to follow its ways that they may find life (8:32–35). Created before all else, it even presides at the creation of all[96] and takes its delight in being among the sons of men (8:22–31). Later on it says that it has "come forth from the mouth of the Most High" (Sir 24:3) in such wise that it can declare that it is the same as the Book of the Covenant and the law of Moses (Sir 24:23 [24:22E]; Bar 4:1). In Solomon's Book of Wisdom possession of the Spirit that penetrates everything is attributed to it (Wis 7:22); it is nothing other than "the refulgence of eternal life, the spotless mirror of God's majesty, and the image of His goodness" (7:26).

2.1.4. AN EVALUATION OF THAT PRIVILEGED RELIGIOUS EXPERIENCE

2.1.4.1. The books of the Prior Testament have been read over and over again and interpreted without cease. They remain the privileged testimonies of those experiences (of Israel) and of that hope briefly set forth above. In the time of Jesus the hope of the Jews took on diverse shapes, according to views prevalent among different groups of political factions. Though the final fulfilment of that hope was regarded as certain, vague indeed remained the modalities of that fulfilment. For instance, Pharisees believed that a Messiah king would come forth from David's line;[97] but in addition to such an anointed king, whose power would be political, Essenes were also awaiting a priestly Messiah (cf. Zech 4:14;

---

[96]L: *universae creationi praesidet;* F: *elle préside à l'apparition de l'univers.*
[97]F: Whereas the Pharisees believed in the coming of a Davidic Messiah.

cf. Lev 4:3), who would take precedence over the former, and even a Prophet, who was to precede both of them (cf. Deut 18:18; 1 Macc 4:46; 14:41).

2.1.4.2. The expectation of God's kingdom, which was to bring salvation to all human beings and radically change the human situation, existed above all as the chief point of the faith and hope of the people of Israel. But its coming, the content of the good news (or gospel),[98] would make Jerusalem arise and enlighten the whole world (Isa 52:7–10). That kingdom, based on equity and justice, would manifest to all human beings the real aspects of the holiness of God, who wants all to be saved (Psalms 93, 96–99). The powers of this world, however, that have usurped the kingly authority of God, would be stripped of their vain titles (Dan 2:31–45). Among the grand manifestations of God's kingship would be especially His victory over human death, to be achieved in resurrection (Isa 26:19; Dan 12:2–3; 2 Macc 7:9, 14; 12:43–45).

It would be the role of John the Baptist to announce the imminent coming of this definitive kingdom, to be inaugurated by one "who is stronger than" he (Mt 3:11–12 and par.). The times would now be fulfilled;[99] everyone who does penance for his sins[100] would be able to experience true salvation (Mk 1:1–8; Mt 3:1–12; Lk 3:1–18).

Chap. 2—The Fulfilment of the Promises of Salvation in Christ Jesus

2.2.1. THE PERSON AND MISSION OF JESUS CHRIST

2.2.1.1. The Gospel Testimony
"When the fulness of time had come" (Gal 4:4), Jesus of Nazareth, "born of a woman, born under the law," arrived on the scene *to bring the hope of Israel to fulfilment*. According to his own words, by his preaching of the gospel "the time has been fulfilled, and the kingdom of God is at hand" (Mk 1:15). In his person *this kingdom is now present and is at work* (cf. Lk 17:21 and the kingdom parables). Miracles mighty deeds performed by him through God's Spirit show that G

---

[98]L: *Adventus autem eius, in quo Boni Nuntii (seu 'Evangelii') materia cont* F: Son avènement, objet d'une Bonne Nouvelle. . . .

[99]L: *tempora iam impleta erunt;* F: *Les temps sont maintenant accomplis.*

[100]F: who repents of his sins.

kingdom has arrived (Mt 12:28). Jesus has come "not to abolish the law and the prophets, but to fulfil them" (Mt 5:17).

Yet this fulfilment *cannot be conceived of as similar to that which the people of his time had derived from the(ir) reading of Scripture.* To appreciate the difference between the two interpretations, one must accurately weigh the testimony of the Gospels. These writings stem from disciples, who were witnesses[101] of his words and deeds (Acts 1:1) and have handed them on to us under the inspiration of the Holy Spirit[102] (2 Tim 3:16; cf. Jn 16:13). The Spirit's activity not only saw to it that this handing on would be done quite faithfully; rather, with the passage of time and through the Spirit-inspired reflection of the sacred writers, it caused the tradition about Jesus' deeds and acts to be expressed *in an ever richer and more developed way.* Thus are to be explained the variety and diversity in the manner of writing, the ideas, and the vocabulary detected, for instance, between the Synoptic Gospels and the Fourth Gospel.[103] Since, however, this recollection and this understanding of Jesus' words have come to maturity in the primitive apostolic community under the guidance of the Holy Spirit, Christians may rightly accept with firm faith these variant representations of Jesus and his message in their differing degrees of development as the authentic word of God, guaranteed by the authority of the Church.

2.2.1.2. *How Jesus Had Recourse to the Tradition of the Prior Testament*

The way Jesus regards not only the law but also the titles ascribed by Scripture to various mediators of salvation depends essentially on the relationship that he enjoys with God, viz. that of a son toward his father (see 2.2.1.3 below).

(a) It is not surprising that he accepted the titles "Master" (Mk 9:5 etc.) and "Prophet" (Mt 16:14; Mk 6:15; Jn 4:19). Indeed, he attributed the latter to himself (Mt 13:57; Lk 13:33). Though he denied that he was

---

[101]F: who lived (through) the experience of his words and his deeds.

[102]F: with the authority of the Holy Spirit.

[103]F: The Spirit's activity did not consist, indeed, merely in insuring a materially faithful transmission; rather it made fertile a reflection that produced in time *an ever richer and more developed expression* of the story of the deeds of Jesus. Whence (come) the differences of tone, conception, and vocabulary that are detected, for instance, between the Synoptics and the Fourth Gospel.

a "king" and a "messiah" in a mere earthly sense (cf. Lk 4:5–7; Jn 6:15), he did not refuse the name "Son of David" (e.g. Mk 10:47 etc.). Indeed, he presented himself as a Davidic king the day he entered Jerusalem with the acclamation of the crowds, in order to fulfil Scripture (Mt 21:1–11; cf. Zech 9:9–10). He conducted himself in the temple as "one having authority," even though he refused to tell the priests with what authority he was acting (Mk 11:15–16, 28). In this case his role actually appeared to be more that of a prophet than of a king (cf. Mk 11:17, where Isa 56:7 and Jer 7:11 are quoted).

(b) Jesus permitted Peter to acknowledge him, in the name of the twelve disciples, as the *Christ* (i.e. the *Messiah*). Yet he immediately forbade (them) to say anything about this to anyone (Mk 8:30 ff.), because such a profession of faith was still very imperfect, and Jesus was already thinking about his own final outcome and death (Mk 8:31 etc.). The way in which he conceived of the Messiah, son of David, differed from the interpretation proposed by the Scribes. This, indeed, becomes evident when he shows them that according to Ps 110:1 that person is actually David's Lord (Mt 22:41–46 and par.). In the Synoptic Gospels, when the high priest inquires of Jesus whether he is the Christ (Messiah), the Son of God (or, of the Blessed One; cf. 2 Sam 7:14; Ps 2:7), Jesus gives an answer in terms that differ according to the individual evangelists (Mk 14:62; Mt 26:64; Lk 22:67–70, where the question itself is even divided into two parts). Yet in the three cases he openly declares that the Son of Man (cf. Dan 7:13–14) will soon sit at the right hand of God (or of the Power), as a king in divine glory. In John's Gospel, when Pontius Pilate, the procurator,[104] interrogates Jesus, whether he is the "King of the Jews," he states that his "kingdom is not of (*ek*) this world," and that he himself has come "to bear witness to the truth" (Jn 18:36–37).[105] In fact, Jesus never presents himself as a lord, but only as a servant, even as one bound in slavery (Mk 10:45; Lk 22:27; Jn 13:13–16).

(c) The title *Son of Man,* which Jesus alone uses of himself in the Gospel texts, is of great importance. It designates him as the mediator of salvation according to the Book of Daniel (cf. 7:13). Yet up to his

---

[104]F: the prefect.
[105]F: he exercises it (his kingship) by "bearing witness to the truth" (Jn 18:36–37).

passion[106] this title remains somewhat ambiguous, because it could sometimes designate the person himself who is speaking, according to a rather frequent expression in Aramaic. Jesus thus conducts himself and speaks in this way as if he is apparently reluctant to reveal explicitly the secret—or rather the mystery—of his person, for people would not yet be able to understand it. According to the Fourth Gospel, Jesus utters only those things that his disciples "can bear" (Jn 16:12).

(d) At the same time, however, Jesus insinuates many things that will only later become clear with the help of the Holy Spirit (Jn 16:13). Thus, at the Last Supper when he utters the words over the cup (Mk 14:24 and par.), he seems to allude to the mission of the *Suffering Servant,* who lays down his life for many (Isa 53:12), as he himself seals a new covenant with his blood (cf. Isa 42:6; Jer 31:31). We may, indeed, think that he already has this in mind when he states that the Son of Man has come "not to be served but to serve and to give his life as a ransom for many" (Mk 10:45).

(e) Still other things, however, are to be considered. For God not only announced His coming through certain human beings, but also by means of divine attributes, viz. through His *Word,* His *Spirit,* and His *Wisdom* (cf. 2.1.3.3. above). In fact, Jesus presented himself speaking in the name and with the authority of the Father, both in the Fourth Gospel (Jn 3:34; 7:16; 8:26; 12:49; 14:24; cf. its Prologue, where he is called the *Logos,* "Word") and in the Synoptics: "You have heard that it was said . . ., but I say to you . . ." (Mt 5:21 ff.; cf. 7:24, 29). Elsewhere he declares that he is speaking and acting *with the Spirit of God* (Mt 12:28), that he possesses this divine power, and that he will send it upon his disciples (Lk 24:49; Acts 1:8; Jn 16:7). Finally, he insinuates that God's *Wisdom* is present and active in himself (Mt 11:19; cf. Lk 11:31).

Thus the two ways, one "from above" and the other "from below," which God in the Prior Testament had prepared for His coming among human beings, are seen to meet in Christ Jesus (see 1.1.11.1): "from above," in that humans are summoned more and more proximately by God's Word, Spirit, and Wisdom;[107] but "from below," in that better and better drawn pictures of a Messiah as a king of justice and peace, of a lowly Suffering Servant, and of a mysterious Son of Man

---

[106]F adds: or at least up to his reply to Caiaphas.
[107]F adds: which descend into our world.

emerge and bring it about that humanity rises, along with them, closer to God Himself. Thus two routes of Christology are opened up: in the one, God reveals Himself in Jesus Christ as one coming among human beings to save them by communicating to them His own life; in the other, the human race finds in Christ, the new Adam, the primordial call to be adoptive children of God.

2.2.1.3. *Jesus' Relationship to God*

(a) The ultimate explanation, or rather the mystery, of Jesus lies essentially in *his filial relation to God*. For in his prayer he addresses God as "Abba"; in Aramaic this word denotes "Father" with a nuance of familiarity (cf. Mk 14:36 etc.). He also gives himself the name "Son" in the very verse in which he affirms that only the Father knows the day of final judgment—not even the angels, nor indeed the Son (Mk 13:32). This mode of presenting himself as "Son" in the presence of "the Father" is found a number of times, either in the Fourth Gospel (e.g. Jn 17:1: "Father, the hour has come; glorify your Son that the Son may glorify you"; cf. also Jn 3:35–36, 5:19–23) or in the so-called Johannine "logion" of the Matthean and Lucan Gospels (Mt 11:25–27 = Lk 10:21–22). This familiar[108] relationship of Jesus with God appears so intimate that he can assert: "All things have been entrusted to me by my Father. No one knows the Son except the Father; nor does anyone know the Father except the Son, and the one to whom the Son chooses to reveal Him" (Mt 11:27; cf. Lk 10:22).

(b) This is the intimate secret from which originate, as though from a spring, all the deeds of Jesus and his mode of conduct—or, to put it another way, this is his *true sonship* (or filial condition).[109] Of this relationship he is conscious even at a young age (Lk 2:49); and he manifests it by his *perfect obedience* to the Father's will (Mk 14:36 and par.). This filial condition does not prevent him from being perfectly human; he is one who "advances in wisdom, age, and grace before God and human beings" (Lk 2:52). Thus he grows more and more in the awareness of the mission entrusted to him by the Father, from his childhood up to his death on the cross. Finally, he experiences death in as cruel a

---

[108]F omits the adjective "familiar."

[109]L adds the parenthetical phrase; F has merely *sa véritable "filialité."*

fashion as any other human would (cf. Mt 26:39; 27:46 and par.); or, as
the Epistle to the Hebrews puts it, "Son though he was, he learned obedience from what he suffered" (5:8).

2.2.1.4. *The Person of Jesus as the Origin of Christology*

Thus we see that all the titles, all the roles and mediatory modes
related to salvation in Scripture have been assumed and united in the person of Jesus. Those who believed in him, however, had to interpret all
these things in an entirely new way. Paradoxically, it turned out that the
kingdom of *the Messiah* (i.e. of the Christ) came into being through the
scandal of the cross, once Jesus had undergone death as God's Suffering
Servant (1 Pet 2:21–25, echoing Isaiah 53) and had entered by his resurrection into the glory of the *Son of Man* (Acts 7:56; Rev 1:13; cf. Dan
7:13–14). Thus he came to be acknowledged in faith as "the Christ, the
Son of David," and also as "the Son of God in power" (Rom 1:3–4),
as "Lord" (Acts 2:36; Phil 2:11, etc.); as "the Wisdom of God" (1 Cor
1:24; cf. Col 1:15–16; Heb 1:3), "the Word" of God[110] (Rev 19:13; 1
Jn 1:1; Jn 1:1–14); "the Lamb of God," slain yet glorified (Rev 5:6 ff.;
Jn 1:29; 1 Pet 1:19), the faithful "Witness" (Rev 1:5), the true "Shepherd" (Jn 10:1 ff.; cf. Ezekiel 34), "the Mediator" of the new covenant,
functioning in a royal "priesthood" (Heb 8:1–10:18); and finally as "the
First and the Last" (Rev 1:17), a title given to God alone in the Prior
Testament (Isa 44:6; 48:12). Thus the Scriptures have come to fulfilment
in Jesus in another and a better way than Israel had ever expected. Yet
this can be apprehended only in an act of faith, by which we acknowledge that he is the Messiah, the Lord, and Son of God (Rom 8:29; Jn
20:31).

2.2.2. THE ORIGINS OF FAITH IN JESUS CHRIST

2.2.2.1. *The Light of Easter*

(a) The faith of Jesus' disciples, even though they had "believed in
him" (cf. Jn 2:11) for a long time, remained very imperfect as long as
he was alive. Indeed, it was completely shattered at his death, as all the
Gospels testify. Yet it emerged more fully and clearly once God raised

---

[110]L: "*Sermo (vel "Verbum") Dei*"; F: "*comme Parole (ou Verbe) de Dieu.*"

him (from the dead) and granted him to be seen by his disciples (Acts 10:40 f.; cf. 1.3; Jn 20:19–29). The appearances, in which Jesus "presented himself alive with many proofs after his passion"[111] (Acts 1:3), were in no way expected by the disciples, with the result that "they accepted the truth of his resurrection only with hesitation" (Leo the Great, *Serm.* 61.4; cf. Mt 28:17; Lk 24:11).

(b) As the light of Easter began to shine, a number of sayings of Jesus that had at first seemed rather obscure became clear (cf. Jn 2:22), as did a number of his deeds (Jn 12:16). But especially the meaning of his passion and death was laid bare, once he himself "opened (their) minds to the understanding of the Scriptures" (Lk 24:32, 35). In this way, then, they were made witnesses (Lk 24:48; Acts 1:8; cf. 1 Cor 15:4–8); their words became the foundation on which the faith of the primitive community was based. Through their testimony all that was written about Jesus "in the law of Moses, the Prophets, and the Psalms" (Lk 24:44) was to be believed. At the same time one could discern how God's promises had come to fulfilment in him.

(c) At the same time such appearances (Acts 10:40–41; Mk 16:12–14) also spelled out the meaning of those events that were seen as the sequel of his resurrection:[112] the gift of the Holy Spirit, given on the evening of Easter itself according to the Fourth Gospel (Jn 20:22), the coming of the same Spirit upon the disciples on the day of Pentecost (Acts 2:16–21, 33), and miracles of healing performed "in the name of Jesus" (Acts 3:6 etc.). From that time on the core of apostolic faith was not only God's kingdom, the coming of which Jesus had announced (Mk 1:15), but even Jesus himself, in whom that kingdom had found its beginning (cf. Acts 8:12; 19:8, etc.)—that Jesus whom the apostles had known before his death and who by his resurrection from the dead had entered into his glory (Lk 24:26; Acts 2:36).

2.2.2.2. *The Development of Christology*
(a) According to Jesus' own promise (Lk 24:49; Acts 1:8), his disciples "were endowed with power, as the Holy Spirit came down upon them," once "the day of Pentecost had come" (Acts 2:1–4; cf. 10:44).

---

[111]F omits the last prepositional phrase.
[112]F adds: from the dead.

This was, in fact, the special gift of the *New Covenant*. Through the former covenant the law had been given to the people of God; by the new one the Spirit of God was poured out upon all flesh according to a prophetic promise (Acts 2:16–21; cf. Joel 3:1–5 LXX). Through his baptism "in the Holy Spirit" (Acts 11:16; cf. Mt 3:11 and par.) the apostles received the morale and the courage to bear witness to Christ (Acts 2:23–26; 10:39, etc.), to proclaim God's word with boldness (*parrhēsia,* Acts 4:29, 31), and to perform miracles in the name of the Lord Jesus (Acts 3:6 etc.). So there came into being the community of believers in Jesus Christ. Later, the Church, built up "in the Holy Spirit" (Acts 9:31; Rom 15:16–19; Eph 2:20–22), so grew among Jews and in the midst of the nations that testimony was borne to Christ and God's kingdom and spread even "to the end of the earth" (Acts 1:8).

(b) The *gospel traditions* were gathered and gradually committed to writing in this light of Easter, until at length they took a fixed form in four booklets. These booklets do not simply contain things "that Jesus began to do and to teach" (Acts 1:1);[113] they also present theological interpretations of such things (cf. the *Instruction of the Pontifical Biblical Commission* of May 14, 1964; *AAS* 56 [1964] 712–18). In these booklets, then, one must learn to look for *the Christology of each evangelist*. This is especially true of John, who in the patristic period would receive the title "Theologian." Similarly, other authors whose writings are preserved in the New Testament have interpreted the deeds and sayings of Jesus in diverse ways, and even more so his death and resurrection. Hence one may speak of the Christology of the Apostle Paul, which develops and takes on new forms from his first letters up to the tradition that issues from him. Still other Christologies are found in the Epistle to the Hebrews, in 1 Peter, in the Book of Revelation, in the Letters of James and Jude, and in 2 Peter, although they do not have the same amount of development in such writings.

These Christologies do not vary among themselves only because of *the differing light* by which they illumine the person of Christ as he fulfils the Prior Testament. But one or other *brings forth new elements,* especially the "infancy narratives" of Matthew and Luke, which teach the virginal conception of Jesus, whereas the mystery of his pre-existence is

---

[113]F: are not simple collections of "what Jesus did and taught."

brought out in the writings of Paul and John. Yet a complete treatise on "Christ the Lord, Mediator, and Redeemer" is nowhere to be found. The New Testament authors, precisely as pastors and teachers, bear witness indeed to the same Christ, but with voices that differ as in the harmony of one piece of music.

(c) *But all these testimonies must be accepted in their totality* in order that Christology, as a form of knowledge about Christ rooted and based in faith, may thrive as true and authentic among believing Christians. An individual may legitimately be inclined to accept this or that testimony because it seems more apt to express the meaning of Christ in a given mentality or culture. But all these testimonies constitute for the faithful the unique gospel proclaimed by Christ and about him. No one of them can be rejected on the grounds that, being the product of a secondary development, it would not express the *true* image of Christ, or on the grounds that, bearing the traces of a bygone cultural context,[114] it would be of no importance today. The interpretation of the texts, which remains quite necessary, should by no means end up by throwing out any of their content.

(d) *The modes of expression used by these (New Testament) authors* in presenting their Christology deserve serious attention. As has already been noted (2.2.1.4), these expressions are very often derived from Scripture itself. Nevertheless, once the gospel message came into contact with various Hellenistic teachings and religions,[115] pastors and teachers of the apostolic period gradually began to adopt prudently terms and figures from the contemporary way of speaking among Gentiles, giving them interpretations consonant with the demands of the faith. Examples of this sort, however, are not numerous (e.g. the word *plērōma* in Col 1:19), but they are not to be ascribed to some false syncretism. For the inspired authors[116] seek in this way to describe the same Christ that others depict with expressions drawn more directly from the Scriptures themselves. But they have thus opened up a way for theologians of all ages who have felt the need, and still feel it, of finding "auxiliary" languages to clarify for the people of their day the special and basic lan-

---

[114]L: *vel quasi in se vestigia impressum ab antiquis culturis imbuta*(?); F: *ou comme si, marquée par un contexte culturel ancien.*

[115]F: Hellenistic philosophies and religions.

[116]This subject is not explicitly expressed in F.

guage of Scripture so that the correct and integral proclamation of the
gospel might be brought to human beings of all ages.[117]

2.2.3. CHRIST AS THE MEDIATOR OF SALVATION

2.2.3.1. *Christ Present in His Church*
(a) Christ remains with his own until the close of the age (Mt 28:20).
The Church, whose entire life is derived from Christ the Lord, has to
carry out this mandate: to plumb the depths of the mystery of Christ and
to make it known to humanity. Yet this can only be done in faith and
under the influence of the Holy Spirit (1 Cor 2:10–11). This Spirit, indeed, apportions His gifts to each one as He wills (cf. 1 Cor 12:11), "for
the building up of the body of Christ, until all of us attain to the unity of
faith and the knowledge of God's Son, to mature manhood, and to the
measure of the stature of the fulness of Christ" (Eph 4:12–13). Thus the
Church, inserted into the world, experiences through its faith Christ present in the midst of it (cf. Mt 18:20). For this reason it strains with a firm
hope toward the glorious coming of the Lord. This is the desire it expresses in prayer, especially when it celebrates the memorial of his passion and resurrection, vigorously calling for his return, "Come, Lord
Jesus" (Rev 22:20; cf. 1 Cor 16:22).
(b) *It is the proper function of the Church to recognize authentically
the presence and activity of Christ* in the diverse situations of human
history. Hence the Church must be concerned to scrutinize "the signs of
the times" and to interpret them in the light of the gospel (cf. *Gaudium
et spes* §4). To do this, the ministers of the gospel and the faithful, each
according to one's proper function, are to *preserve the doctrine of God,*
our Savior (Titus 2:10), and "guard the deposit" (1 Tim 6:20), lest they
"be carried about with every wind of teaching" (Eph 4:14). Therefore
true faith in Christ, authentic activity of the Holy Spirit, and correct
"praxis" of faithful Christians must always undergo "discernment" (1
Cor 12:10) and "testing" (1 Jn 4:1).
True faith is faith in Jesus Christ, the Son of God, who has come
"in the flesh" (1 Jn 4:2), who has revealed to human beings the name
of the Father (Jn 17:6), who "has given himself as a ransom for all" (1

---

[117]F: in order to proclaim the gospel in its fulness correctly to all.

Tim 2:6; cf. Mk 10:45 and par.), who rose[118] on the third day (1 Cor 15:4), who has been taken up into glory (1 Tim 3:16), who sits at God's right hand (1 Pet 3:22), and whose glorious coming is awaited at the end of time (Titus 2:13). A Christology that would not profess all these things would be departing from the testimony of apostolic tradition, the ultimate rule of faith according to St. Irenaeus (*Dem. apost.* §3): "the rule of truth," preserved in all the churches by the succession of the apostles (*Adv. haer.* 3.1,2) and received by every Christian in baptism (ibid. 1.9,4).

(c) Similarly, *the activity of the Holy Spirit* is to be discerned with the help of sure signs. The Church is led by God's Spirit along its paths. But just like anyone of the faithful (Rom 8:14), it cannot "put credence in every spirit" (1 Jn 4:1). For the Spirit of God is none other than "the Spirit of Jesus" (Acts 16:7), that (Spirit) without whom no one can say "Jesus is Lord" (1 Cor 12:3). This same Spirit brings to disciples' minds[119] all that Jesus has said (Jn 14:26) and guides them into all the truth (Jn 16:13), until the "words of God" (*Dei verbum* §8) are brought to fulfilment in the Church.

Through this Spirit the Father has raised Jesus from the dead (Rom 8:11) that He might create in him a new being "in true righteousness and holiness" (Eph 4:24 [*RSV*]). Through the same (Spirit) God will raise up all those who have believed in Christ (Rom 8:11; 1 Cor 6:14). Through faith and baptism (1 Cor 6:15) Christians become members of Christ and are united with him even in their bodies, which share in his life and become the temple of the Holy Spirit (1 Cor 6:19). Thus all make up only one body, which is the crucified and risen body of Christ himself. This body, animated by one Spirit (1 Cor 12:12 ff.; Eph 4:4), assumes all the baptized as its members: so the Church is constituted (Col 1:24; Eph 1:22). Christ is the head of this body, which he vivifies and to which he gives growth (Col 2:19) by the "power" of his Spirit (Eph 4:16). This is "the new creature" (2 Cor 5:17; Gal 6:15)[120] in which Christ reconciles all that sin had divided. He reconciles human beings with one another (Eph 2:11–18), sinners with God, enemies of whom they had become through disobedience (2 Cor 5:18–20; Rom 5:10; Col

---

[118]F: *qui est resuscité*; 1 Cor 15:4 reads *egēgertai* (RSV: "was raised").
[119]F: recalls.
[120]F: the new creation.

1:21), and even the whole universe, in which Christ has vanquished the powers of evil oppressing humanity (Col 1:20; 2:15; Eph 1:10, 20–22).

2.2.3.2. *The Total Christ As the Goal of All Things*

(a) *The salvation brought by Christ must, therefore, be termed "total,"* for it touches human beings even in their bodies (Rom 6:3–4; Col 2:11–12) through the grace of Baptism, of the Eucharist (cf. 1 Cor 10:16–17), and of the other sacraments. The holiness of Christ, communicated to the Church, thus flows into the very life of Christians that through them it may reach the world in which they dwell. In imitation of their "first-born" brother (Rom 8:29), they participate in the building up of God's kingdom, which Christ came to establish among human beings, proposing his program of love, justice, and peace (Gal 5:22–23; Phil 4:8; Col 3:12–15). Following the example given by the Master, they too are "to lay down their lives for the brethren" (1 Jn 3:16).

Since Jesus has been sent to preach the gospel to the poor, to release captives, and to set at liberty those oppressed (Lk 4:18–21), his disciples must be concerned to continue this task of liberation. Thus his Church prepares for the coming of Christ's definitive kingdom, in which he will have subjected all things to himself and then subject himself to his Father, "that God may be all to all" (1 Cor 15:28). That this goal may be attained, the Church as of now inserts itself into this world through its members. Far from ordering them to leave this world, it works through them so that the spirit of the gospel may be able to penetrate into all its structures, familial, social, and political. Thus Christ, present in the affairs of this world, pours forth his salvific grace upon them. He "who has descended into the lower parts of the earth" and "has been raised above all the heavens" now "fills all things" (Eph 4:9–10).

(b) None of this can happen without toil and suffering (Mt 5:11; Jn 15:20; 16:33; Col 1:24). Sin that has already entered this world from the beginning (Rom 5:12) continues to wreak its havoc in it. God's kingdom, though already inaugurated, has not yet been fully manifested. Little by little it advances with the pangs, as it were, of a woman in travail (Mt 24:8; Jn 16:21–22). What has been created[121] has been subjected to futility and awaits freedom from the bondage to corruption (Rom 8:19–

---

[121]L: *creatura ipsa;* F: *La création elle-même.*

21). But Christ by his death and resurrection has triumphed over sin; he has overcome "the prince of this world" (Jn 12:31; 16:11, 33). Therefore Christians, taking their cue from him and sustained by his grace, have to do battle and suffer even unto martyrdom and death, if this be called for (Mt 24:9–13 and par.; Jn 16:2; Rev 6:9–11), that good may triumph over evil, until there arrive "the new heavens and the new earth, wherein righteousness dwells" (2 Pet 3:13).

Then He who loved us first (1 Jn 4:19) will be acknowledged, loved, and worshiped; he will be served by all human beings, who will become His adoptive children (Eph 1:5). So will his salvific activity come to its term in blessed eternity. For God Himself with mercy, fidelity, and indefatigable patience (Rom 2:4–5; 3:25–26; 9:22) is pursuing it, ever since His first summons, from which humanity chose to withdraw, even to the day when all will enjoy unending happiness and will acclaim Him: "To Him who sits on the throne and to the Lamb be blessing, honor, glory, and power for ever and ever" (Rev 5:13).

COMMENTARY

This document on Christology has been issued by the Pontifical Biblical Commission, which in 1971 was associated by Pope Paul VI with the Sacred Congregation for the Doctrine of the Faith.[122] Cardinal Joseph Ratzinger, the head of the Congregation, is *ex officio* president of the Commission. Though formerly composed of cardinals as members, who were aided by a number of consultants, the Commission has since 1971 been made up of 20 biblical scholars from across the world. Until March 1984 the Commission was composed of the following priest-scholars:[123] José Alonso Díaz, S.J. (Spain), Jean Dominique Barthélemy, O.P. (France/Switzerland), Pierre Benoit, O.P. (France/Israel), Henri Cazelles, S.S. (France), Guy Couturier, C.S.C. (Canada), Alfons Deissler (Germany), Bp. Albert Descamps (Belgium), Jacques Dupont, O.S.B. (Belgium), Joachim Gnilka (Germany), John Greehy (Ireland), Pierre Grelot (France), Augustyn Jankowski, O.S.B. (Poland), Carlo Maria Martini, S.J. (Italy), Antonio Moreno Casamitjana (Chile), Laurent Naré (Upper Volta), Angelo Penna (Italy), Ignace de la Potterie, S.J. (Belgium/Italy), Jerome D. Quinn (U.S.A.), Matthew Vellanickal (India), Benjamin Wambacq, O.Praem. (Belgium). The staff secretary was Marino Maccarelli, O.S.M. The document on Christology was prepared by these members and was voted on by fifteen of them in April 1983.[124]

---

[122]For further details about the history of the Commission and the revamping of it by Pope Paul VI, see my account in *A Christological Catechism* 97–103; cf. "Sedula cura," *AAS* 63 (1971) 665–69.

[123]*Annuario pontificio 1984* (Vatican City: Editrice Vaticana, 1984) 1112. New members were appointed on March 22, 1984; see *CBQ* 46 (1984) 524.

[124]C. M. Martini, S.J., had been a member until he became a cardinal (1983) as archbishop of Milan. Two had died: Bp. A. Descamps (Belgium), former secretary, and A. Penna (Italy). Two were absent due to ill health: J. Alonso Díaz, S.J., and J. D. Quinn.

The text appears without papal approval, unlike the Instruction of 1964 approved by Pope Paul VI. This, of course, raises a question about the authority to be accorded to this document, especially when one recalls the debate and the official declaration about the authority of the Commission's *responsa* in the early part of this century.[125] But this difference is part of the revamping of the Commission as of 1971. Neither the Commission's earlier text, *Fede e cultura alla luce della Bibbia*,[126] nor the document on Christology issued by the International Theological Commission (1981)[127] was issued with papal approval.

The preface of the Biblical Commission's document states that its purpose is not to engage in exegesis or catechetics. The Commission's mandate has been to promote biblical studies within the Roman Catholic Church and to aid the Church's magisterium, pastors, and faithful in biblical matters. In issuing this document, the Commission is replying to a question about the Christ-Messiah, posed by whom it is not said.

In the main the document does two things. Its first part (28 pages in each language) surveys eleven approaches to Christology used in modern times, points out the advantages of each as well as the risks they run, and asks the question: How can such risks be avoided? The answer: By the principle of totality—one must listen to the *total* biblical testimony about Christ. The second part (20 pages in each language) presents a global sketch of the biblical testimony to Christ: the OT promises and mediatory roles of salvation; and the fulfilment of these in the person of Jesus Christ in the NT. The survey of the eleven approaches to Christology and the critique of them are neither drawn out nor extensive. Some readers may find both the survey and the critique too brief or cryptic, indeed even unsatisfactory. But the importance of the document lies not in these preliminary sections 1 and 2 of Part I, which are often quite dense.

The importance of the document is found rather in two things: first, the insistence on the total biblical picture of Christ, which some of the approaches have not always respected (see section 3 of Part I). In stressing this total Christological picture, the Commission cites many passages

---

[125]See *A Christological Catechism* 98 n. 4.
[126]*Atti della sessione plenaria 1979 della Pontificia Commissione Biblica*, ed. D. Barthélemy (Turin: Elle di Ci, 1981).
[127]*Select Questions on Christology* (Washington: USCC, 1980).

from the OT and NT that have often been used in the past in one way or another; but its attempt to present them globally and the new emphasis given to certain passages are welcome indeed.

Second, what is of even greater importance in the document is the interspersing of comments throughout it about the proper methodological interpretation of Scripture itself and of cautions about the disregard of modern exegetical studies. The document avoids all harmonization of the biblical data and insists on the recognition of the various Christologies in the individual Gospels and other NT writings.

Nowhere in the document does the Commission speak of the historical-critical method of biblical interpretation, but in many places its mode of interpreting both the OT and NT is in accord with the principles of that methodology. I have culled from the document as a whole a number of specific comments which reveal the Commission's own critical approach to Scripture. These come mainly from section 2 of Part I, in which the risks of the eleven approaches are being discussed. But it is also clear that such a methodology is not for the Commission an end in itself, but only a means to arrive at what it calls "an integral Christology." It is important to note this aspect of the Commission's reference to "the demands of biblical criticism" (1.2.7.2), since the Commission is also aware of "critical hypotheses that are always subject to revision" (1.2.10). Obviously, the Commission is not equating its own view of proper "biblical criticism" with such hypotheses.

In this regard some of the more important comments of the Commission may be noted here. It expresses the desideratum that biblical studies be conducted with the aid of the exegetical methods of our day and that they become more advanced in research and investigation than they are at present (1.3.3). The Commission mentions specifically certain problems that need such study: the composition-process of the biblical books, the neglect of which can only lead to a superficial reading of Scripture, even to a would-be "theological" reading that is setting off on a deceptive route (ibid.). The Commission calls for an openness to critical questions in exegesis (1.2.1.2) and recognizes that the historicity of the Gospel episodes cannot be pressed in their "minute details," since the latter may play only a theological role in literary composition; nor can the word-for-word authenticity of Jesus' sayings be too readily insisted on, given the different forms that they often take (ibid.). "The demands of biblical criticism and the multiplicity of the NT Christologies" are to be respected (1.2.7.2; see also 1.2.10). The Commission insists that the Jesus of history must be admitted as "the origin of Christology" (1.2.8.1); Christology is not simply born of faith in the Easter kerygma (ibid.). It also stresses that one cannot take merely the "older" NT texts as "the only trustworthy ones" in the study of Christology, as if the more recent texts were merely "speculations born of a later period that have completely changed the 'original' data coming from 'the historical Jesus' " (1.2.7.3). Though the language of the NT may be "symbolic" and in this way pass on to us the Easter kerygma, that symbolic character cannot simply be reduced to something "mythological" (1.2.8.2). The Commission frankly admits that the resurrection of Christ "cannot be proved in an empirical way. For by it Jesus was introduced into 'the world to come' " (1.2.6.2). Since "elements in the Prior Testament that are preparatory" to Christ and his work may not be "dismissed or so belittled that the New Testament is deprived of its roots," it is desirable that "exegetical studies find a more precise and well-defined place in the study of revelation, which from the beginning and through the whole course of its development has been tending toward its ultimate goal in the totality of the mystery of Christ" (1.2.10). Finally, the Commission has made an important distinction about the use of language in Christology. It considers the formulations of subsequent conciliar definitions to be examples of "auxiliary" language, used when the NT data about Christ have been reconceptualized or reformulated. Such language is not always preferable to the "referential" language of the inspired writers (1.2.2.1), which is "the ultimate source of revelation" about Christ and which is scarcely "less accurate" or "less suited to setting forth a doctrine in well-defined terms" (1.2.1.1). I have culled these comments from the document and in effect have wrenched them from their contexts in order to highlight the significance of them. The reader will do well to consult them in their proper contexts.

In what follows I propose to comment on the different parts of the document. It will be clear that Part II calls for less comment than Part I, and that the latter receives for this reason more extended remarks. It is the dense part of the document. A few further preliminary observations, however, are needed.

In section 1 of Part I, where the modern approaches to Christology are surveyed, the survey is not as factual or as descriptive as it might have been. Value judgments and interpretative remarks are sometimes inserted into this section which should have been relegated to section 2, which is professedly critical. In the commentary that follows I shall take up each approach, summarize or expand the Commission's description (as may be needed), and then join immediately to this summary the Commission's reaction to the approach. The numbering system of the document will be used to indicate the source of the description or reaction.

This document is further remarkable in that it includes the names of some modern exponents of the different approaches. But it has supplied no references, which is understandable in a document of this sort and length. In order to facilitate further study of the document, I shall give some bibliographical references to the writings of the persons named—to the extent that I can. But it must be remembered that it is I who am supplying the references; I cannot guarantee that my identification of the writings will always be what the Commission had in mind.

APPROACH 1:
THE CLASSICAL OR TRADITIONAL TRACT
DE VERBO INCARNATO

This approach is based on conciliar definitions and patristic or medieval theological writings. Today it often makes some use of biblical studies, is influenced by the idea of salvation history, and takes into account recent investigations of Jesus' knowledge and personality. The document refers to such writers as J. Galot[128] and J. Maritain[129] as representatives of this approach (1.1.1.1).

This approach, however, runs the risk of preferring conciliar, patristic, or medieval theological language to that of the NT, as if the language of "this ultimate source of revelation" about Christ were "less accurate or less suited" to a modern Christology (1.2.1.1). Two things

---

[128]E.g. *La personne du Christ: Recherche ontologique* (Gembloux: Duculot, 1969); *La conscience de Jésus* (Gembloux: Duculot, 1971); *Vers une nouvelle christologie* (Gembloux: Duculot, 1971); *Gesu liberatore: Christologia II* (Florence: Fiorentina, 1978); *Le problème christologique actuel* (Chambray les Tours: C. L. D., 1979); *Le Christ, foi et contestation* (Chambray les Tours: C. L. D., 1981).

[129]*On the Grace and Humanity of Jesus* (New York: Herder and Herder, 1969) 89–125.

in particular seem to be criticized in it: (1) the viewing of conciliar or church formulations of doctrine as somehow superior to the formulation of Scripture itself (recall the comment above about "auxiliary" language); (2) the failure to recognize that these conciliar or later theological formulations have not only reformulated but even reconceptualized the biblical data and thus present them in a philosophical construct[130] that cannot claim in Christology the same value as the language or conception of the "ultimate source of revelation."

When Chalcedon taught that Christ "as the one and the same Son . . . perfect in divinity and perfect in humanity, the same truly God and truly man . . . must be acknowledged in two natures, without confusion or change, without division or separation," that "this distinction between the natures was never abolished by their union, but rather the character proper to each of the two natures was preserved as they come together in one person (*prosōpon*) and one hypostasis," and that Christ "is not split or divided into two persons, but is one and the same only-begotten Son, God the Word, the Lord Jesus Christ. . . . ,"[131] it took the NT data and cast them into a philosophical construct or setting that they did not have in the NT itself. In introducing *physis,* "nature," *prosōpon,* "person," and *hypostasis,* "subsistent being," Chalcedon used "auxiliary" language in coping with Nestorianism and Eutychianism.

Moreover, this classical approach runs the risk of appealing to Scripture merely to bolster up or defend its traditional formulation and of not being sufficiently open to the exegetical problems that a critical reading of Scripture calls for today. For instance, this approach often works with a simplistic understanding of the historicity of Gospel narratives or with the word-for-word authenticity of sayings attributed to Jesus in the canonical Gospels. As a result, this approach is often marked with a concern for conservative opinions in biblical interpretation, which are themselves actually quite controversial. In this last view (1.2.1.2) the Commission is pointing its critical finger at Catholic fundamentalism, often associated with this approach to Christology. An example of

---

[130]Such a construct was often born of controversy or designed to counter an erroneous, even heretical, teaching.

[131]*The Christian Faith in the Doctrinal Documents of the Catholic Church* (rev. ed., ed.: J. Neuner and J. Dupuis; Staten Island/Alba, 1982) 154–55 (slightly corrected).

this sort of use of the NT would be the appeal to Jn 10:30, "I and the Father are one," to establish the divinity of Christ.[132]

APPROACH 2:
SPECULATIVE APPROACH OF A CRITICAL TYPE

A more modern systematic Christology applies to conciliar definitions and patristic or medieval formulations the critical mode of reading used by many modern biblical scholars. Such definitions and formulations have to be judged in the light of "the historical and cultural context" from which they come. The reformulations and reconceptualizations were once needed to preserve the content of faith in Christ in the heat of controversy (e.g. with Monophysitism), but proponents of this sort of systematic Christology insist today that those formulas are themselves time-conditioned and have to be scrutinized anew in the light of the basic biblical data. The document names P. Schoonenberg as one of those who have undertaken such a critical scrutiny of Christological teaching (1.1.2.1–3).[133]

Schoonenberg, after expressing six difficulties that the classical approach to Christology based on Chalcedon encounters, proposed a new way of interpreting the personal unity of Jesus Christ, or his God-man relationship. Schoonenberg sees Jesus as a full "human person," and he prefers to speak of the *enhypostasia* (in-hypostatization) of the Word in Jesus the man rather than of the classical *enhypostasia* of Jesus in the Word. For him, the Logos becomes person, acquiring its way of subsisting in salvation history, and becomes a self over against the "thou"

[132]See A. C. Cotter, *Theologia fundamentalis* (2nd ed.; Weston, Mass.: Weston College, 1947) 217–25, esp. 223–24; J. Galot, *Who Is Christ: A Theology of the Incarnation* (Chicago: Franciscan Herald, 1980) 99; *La conscience de Jésus* 159.—For a more balanced interpretation of this verse, see R. E. Brown, *The Gospel according to John (i–xii)* (AB 29; Garden City, N.Y.: Doubleday, 1966) 403, 407; cf. T. E. Pollard, "The Exegesis of John x. 30 in the Early Trinitarian Controversies," *NTS* 3 (1956–57) 334–49.

[133]E.g. *Hy is een God van Mensen: Twee theologische Studies* ('s-Hertogenbosch: Malmberg, 1969) 66–86; *The Christ: A Study of the God-Man Relationship in the Whole of Creation and in Jesus Christ* (New York: Herder and Herder, 1971); "Denken über Chalkedon," *TQ* 160 (1980) 103–7; "Alternativen der heutigen Christologie," *TPQ* 128 (1980) 349–57; "Arianische Christologie? Antwort an J. Galot," *Theologie der Gegenwart* 23 (1980) 50–56.

of the Father only in the Incarnation. In this way Schoonenberg believes that he can better account for the unified human activity of the earthly Jesus, his acquired knowledge, etc., i.e. as they are presented in the NT accounts.

The Commission recognizes the validity of such a critical approach to the time-conditioned formulations of theologians and councils (1.2.2) and refrains from ruling it out. But it asks whether it would not be better to speak of Jesus' " 'human personality,' in the sense in which the scholastics used to speak of his 'individual' and 'singular human nature' " (1.1.2.3 [in effect, a value judgment introduced into the descriptive survey]). Moreover, the Commission cautions that two considerations must temper this sort of critical approach. First, it introduces the distinction between "auxiliary" and "referential" language (1.2.2.1) already noted. And, though it acknowledges the continuity between the basic experience of the apostolic Church, expressed in the NT ("the absolute"), and the subsequent formulation of the Church as a result of its own experience, the Commission is concerned that the new distinctions and analyses of such critical investigations do not do away with the express affirmations of Scripture itself. In this regard one could cite some of the criticism leveled against Schoonenberg's proposal. For example, T. E. Clarke once queried in a review, "Is his quarrel not so much with Chalcedon as with the prologue of John, i.e., with the very possibility of a genuine Incarnation as the primary and incomprehensible instance of the compatibility of the human and the divine?"[134]

Second, the Commission is concerned lest this critical approach to Christology absolutize modern "modes of thinking and speaking," which might call in question the NT understanding of Christ or subject the NT data to a selective process or a certain philosophy that could disturb the balance of the entire biblical picture of Christ itself. One-sided explanations have to be guarded against lest the equilibrium of the testimony not be preserved in all its variety (1.2.2.2). To this aspect of modern Christology the Commission will return in section 3.

---

[134]Review of *The Christ, TS* 33 (1972) 378.

APPROACH 3:
CHRISTOLOGY AND HISTORICAL RESEARCH

This is the approach of so-called *Leben-Jesu-Forschung*. The reconstruction of the life, ministry, and consciousness of Jesus of Nazareth, based on the Gospels considered as historical documents and apart from any later dogmatic formulations, began at the end of the 18th century and developed under the impact of 19th-century historical studies. Noteworthy was the influence of Leopold von Ranke (1795–1886) and Theodor Mommsen (1817–1903), especially the former's emphasis on the study of original sources and his concern to present the past *wie es eigentlich gewesen* ("how it really was").[135] This approach to Christ actually began with H.S. Reimarus (1694–1768), a deist biblical critic who had composed a work attacking historical Christianity (*Apologie oder Schutzschrift für die vernünftigen Verehrer*), which he withheld from publication during his lifetime. Eventually, G. E. Lessing published seven parts of it in 1774–78 as the *Wolfenbüttel Fragmente*.[136] The "Life of Jesus Research" was continued by H. E. G. Paulus (1761–1851),[137] D. F. Strauss (1808–74),[138] J. E. Renan (1823–92),[139] and others.[140] This approach was also adopted by liberal Protestant theologians who sought to substitute "a critically established 'biblical' theology for a 'dogmatic' theology," since the latter seemed to them "to exclude all positive investigation" (1.1.3.1). In this connection the Commission cites the work of the patrologist and church historian A. von Harnack (1851–1930), who,

---

[135]*Geschichte der romanischen und germanischen Völker von 1494 bis 1514: Zur Kritik neuerer Geschichtschreiber* (Sämmtliche Werke 33–34; 3rd ed.; Leipzig: Duncker & Humblot, 1885) vii ("er will bloss zeigen, wie es eigentlich gewesen"). I am indebted to J. P. von Arx, S.J., for this reference.

[136]See *Reimarus: Fragments*, ed. C. H. Talbert (Lives of Jesus series; Philadelphia: Fortress, 1970); H. S. Reimarus, *The Goal of Jesus and His Disciples*, ed. G. W. Buchanan (Leiden: Brill, 1970).

[137]*Das Leben Jesu, als Grundlage einer reinen Geschichte des Urchristentums* (2 vols.; Heidelberg: Winter, 1828).

[138]*The Life of Jesus Critically Examined*, ed. P. C. Hodgson (Lives of Jesus series; Philadelphia: Fortress, 1972).

[139]*The Life of Jesus*, tr. C. E. Wilbour (New York: Carleton, 1864).

[140]This document mentions only these four authors; for others see A. Schweitzer, *The Quest of the Historical Jesus: A Critical Study of Its Progress from Reimarus to Wrede* (London: Black, 1910).

though he reacted against the earlier historical studies of Jesus, did not abandon their methodology or approach; he insisted rather that many of them had too hastily and uncritically rejected traditional and correct views of the origin and development of the NT and of the early Church. In his celebrated book *Das Wesen des Christentums*[141] he himself depicted Jesus as a Galilean ethical teacher who preached about God as Father, about other human beings as brothers, and about the infinite value of the human soul.

In its survey of this "Life of Jesus Research," the Commission recalls the reactions of A. Schweitzer (1875–1965) to the results of this research and investigation.[142] Schweitzer showed that such historical investigation of the life of Jesus did not rise from a purely historical interest in him, but from "the struggle against the tyranny of dogma"; he noted that the greatest lives of Jesus of this sort (by Reimarus and Strauss) had been "written with hate," "not so much hate of the Person of Jesus as of the supernatural nimbus with which it was so easy to surround him." Schweitzer ended his study by stressing the impasse to which the conflicting pictures of Jesus produced by this mode of study actually led. For it yielded no real clarity about the historical Jesus of Nazareth. Schweitzer had his own eschatological interpretation of Jesus, but that does not really belong to this approach and need not concern us here.

Roman Catholic interpreters were also caught up in this sort of historical investigation of Jesus of Nazareth. In mentioning their reactions to it, however, the Commission passes over all too quickly details that would be important for a proper appreciation of the problems that this approach caused within the Catholic Church, entrenched as it was in its battle against Modernism. On the one hand, the Commission acknowledges that M.-J. Lagrange, O.P. (1855–1938), "firmly established 'the historical method' " or "firmly posited the principle of the historical method" (1.1.3.1). But it passes over in silence the troubles that Lagrange encountered within the Church because of his book *La méthode historique*[143] and other writings. As a matter of fact, the principle itself

[141]See *What Is Christianity? Sixteen Lectures Delivered in the University of Berlin during the Winter Term 1899–1900* (London: Williams & Norgate, 1901).

[142]See n. 140 above.

[143]Edition augmentée (EBib; Paris: Lecoffre, 1904); *Historical Criticism and the Old Testament* (London: Catholic Truth Society, 1905).

was already firmly established apart from Lagrange. His contribution was to show that that principle could be properly used by Roman Catholic interpreters. This he did in the face of much opposition from reactionary elements in the Church, and even from the Consistorial Congregation.[144] On the other hand, the Commission now frankly recognizes that the problems associated with the "Life of Jesus Research" were then skirted in Roman Catholic circles only by those writers who naively reiterated "the integral 'historical' truth of everything, even the most minute details found in the Gospel texts" (1.1.3.1). This attitude the Commission ascribes to H. Didon (1840–1900)[145] and E. LeCamus (1839–1906).[146]

Yet not all Roman Catholic involvement in the "Life of Jesus Research" was that reactionary. A somewhat nuanced use of this method of historical study was used by J. Lebreton, M.-J. Lagrange himself, A. Fernández, F. Prat, and G. Ricciotti, all of whom penned so-called Lives of Christ (1.1.3.1).[147] But at the same time all of them had to cope with the *responsa* of the early Biblical Commission: on the Johannine authorship and the historical character of the Fourth Gospel; the authorship, composition, and historical nature of the Synoptic Gospels; the Synoptic relationship (e.g. the rejection of the Two-Source Theory).[148] Those *responsa* cast a dark cloud of fear over Catholic biblical studies in the first part of this century and induced a mentality of suspicion about any kind of critical or historical study of the Gospels and the NT—a mentality that

---

[144]"Decretum de quibusdam rei biblicae commentariis in Sacra Seminaria non admittendis," *AAS* 4 (1912) 530–31. This decree was issued specifically against an introduction to the OT written by K. Holzhey; it includes a vague statement about commentaries of "similar spirit," "ceu scripta plura P. Lagrange" (without further specification). Cf. L.-H. Vincent, "Le Père Lagrange," *RB* 47 (1938) 321–54; "Père Lagrange," *Blackfriars* 19 (1938) 397–411, 475–86.

[145]*Jesus Christ: Our Saviour's Person, Mission and Spirit* (2 vols.; New York: Appleton, 1891).

[146]*The Life of Christ* (3 vols.; New York: Cathedral Library Association, 1906–8; repr., St. Paul: Catechetical Guild, 1945).

[147]J. Lebreton, *The Life & Teaching of Jesus Christ Our Lord* (2 vols.; London: Burns, Oates & Washbourne, 1935); A. Fernández, *The Life of Christ* (Westminster, Md.: Newman, 1958); F. Prat, *Jesus Christ: His Life, His Teaching, and His Work* (2 vols.; Milwaukee: Bruce, 1950); G. Ricciotti, *The Life of Christ* (Milwaukee: Bruce, 1947). The most nuanced of these Lives was that of M.-J. Lagrange, who even avoided "Life" in the title, *The Gospel of Jesus Christ* (2 vols.; London: Burns, Oates & Washbourne, 1938).

[148]See *Enchiridion biblicum* (3rd ed.; Naples: d'Auria, 1956) 187–89, 388–405; *Rome and the Study of Scripture* (7th ed.; St. Meinrad: Grail, 1962) 187–89, 383–400.

still persists among many pastors, teachers, and faithful in the Church today.

In its survey the Commission further recognizes that the historical method itself has undergone scrutiny in recent decades, even a form of self-scrutiny on the part of historians. They have called in question "the 'positivistic' conception of objectivity" once pursued in such investigation (1.1.3.2). (The further paragraphs of this descriptive section, a-c, are, in effect, critiques of the method and really belong with 1.2.3; see below).

In assessing the risks of this historical-method approach to Christology, the Commission admits that Jesus of Nazareth is as apt a subject for historical investigation as any other human being of ancient times. One cannot, then, disregard what historical research "has uncovered about the circumstances" of time and place or other details that have been learned and passed on about him (1.2.3). It further admits the necessity of such historical investigation "lest Jesus be regarded as a mere mythological hero," or "the recognition of him as Messiah and Son of God," which is not a conclusion drawn from such investigation but a recognition of faith, "be reduced to some irrational fideism" (1.1.3.3). This is subtle and has to be properly understood, since the Commission is hinting at those concrete details in the life of Jesus of Nazareth that would have ultimately led contemporaries and disciples to such a recognition of faith. The Commission has no interest in an apotheosized Christ divested of all links with a person of ancient Palestinian history.

However, the Commission also points out problems that have surfaced in the pursuit of the historical method itself (1.1.3.2 a–c) and in the specific application of it to the case of Jesus of Nazareth (1.2.3,1–2). As for the method itself, the objectivity pursued in it is not that of the natural sciences, since the subject being studied involves human experience (social, psychological, and cultural). Hence it can never be adequately reconstructed or reproduced, as one might check a physical experiment by repeating it. Historical investigation is per se limited to *traces* of past events or persons, to testimonies about them in ancient monuments or documents. Moreover, every historical person or event so studied is itself enshrouded in varying degrees of subjectivity, for which the historian must make due allowance. The historian must also cope with his own subjective interest and the attention that slants his study, since he invariably brings to the matter under investigation his own *Vor-*

verständnis, "prejudgment," which can even include a view of life itself and its meaning.[149]

In applying this method of investigation to Jesus of Nazareth, one has to pay special attention to the character of the ancient documents that seem to tell us most about him as a figure in history. One can almost count on the fingers of one hand the ancient extrabiblical testimonies to him (from Suetonius, Pliny the Younger, Tacitus, Lucian, Josephus, and a Baraita of the Babylonian Talmud).[150] Such documents tell us very little. The majority of the ancient testimony, however, comes to us from the books of the NT, and they cannot be read merely as a scholar might read other ancient documents, since that would be to disregard the faith character and the propaganda purpose of these writings. Especially the Gospels have to be so understood, since they come to us as products of early Christian faith and have been composed to arouse faith in God and His Son, Jesus Christ (with the aid of the Holy Spirit). It is not that their faith character makes them unhistorical; they yield, indeed, *traces* of the historical Jesus of Nazareth, but they are traces overlaid with the faith dimension which the professional historian usually regards as beyond his concern in establishing *wie es eigentlich gewesen.*
"how it really was"

APPROACH 4:
CHRISTOLOGY AND THE HISTORY OF RELIGIONS

A refinement of the historical-method approach to Christology came in with the study of the history of religions, i.e. with the comparative study of religions (1.1.4). This approach, though conducted with the concerns of genuine investigation, not only tries to cope with subjective and/or numinous aspects of past human religious experience (e.g. customs, beliefs, rites, etc.), but also studies the influence of one religion on another. Hence its interest in possible syncretism. This mode of study was applied in the 19th century to the Jewish and Christian reli-

---

[149]The Commission refers to H. G. Gadamer, probably to his *Truth and Method* (New York: Seabury, 1975) 235–67, 460–91. See further X. Léon-Dufour, *The Gospels and the Jesus of History* (New York/Tournai: Desclée, 1968) 28–30.

[150]References to these testimonies can be found in my booklet *A Christological Catechism* (see n. 3 above) 11–12.

gions, especially because of the great archeological discoveries in the areas of Egyptology and Assyriology and of the ethnological investigations of anthropologists.

The cultures, laws, myths, and religions of ancient Egypt and Mesopotamia, neighboring countries to west and east of Israel, remained a closed book until the decipherment of ancient Egyptian and Akkadian texts. The study of the Bible in preceding centuries had been conducted almost without concern for the historical matrix of its different writings. That, however, changed with decipherment of the Rosetta Stone (for Egyptian) and of the Rock of Behistun (for Akkadian, i.e. Assyrian-Babylonian cuneiform).

The Rosetta Stone, containing a decree composed in 196 B.C. by Ptolemy V Epiphanes and written "in the sacred writing (= hieroglyphs), in the native script (= Demotic), and in Greek letters," was found in 1799 by an officer of Napoleon's expedition to the western Nile Delta. Its hieroglyphic text was eventually deciphered, mainly by Jean François Champollion in 1822, who later composed an Egyptian grammar and dictionary. He thus opened up the world of Egyptian history, literature, mythology, and religion.

The Rock of Behistun, containing a many-columned inscription recording the victory of Darius the Great over rebels, Gaumata and his followers, and written in Old Persian, Elamite, and Akkadian (all cuneiform scripts), had been known for centuries. But it was only deciphered through the efforts of the Englishman H. C. Rawlinson and especially the German scholar G. F. Grotefend (between 1815 and 1846). The work of Rawlinson and Grotefend thus opened up the world of Assyrian and Babylonian history, literature, laws, mythology, and religion (1.1.4.2).

As a result of these discoveries and decipherments, the world of the Hebrew and Aramaic Scriptures was at last seen properly against its ancient Near Eastern background (once the notorious Babel-Bibel disputes had died down).[151] Though the Commission does not mention it, the dis-

---

[151]Further information on the impact of these archeological and literary discoveries can be found in W. F. Albright, *From the Stone Age to Christianity* (2nd ed.; Garden City, N.Y.: Doubleday, 1957) 25–81; J. Finegan, *Light from the Ancient Past* (Princeton: Princeton University, 1951); R. E. Brown, *Recent Discoveries and the Biblical World* (Wilmington, Del.: Glazier, 1983).

covery of the Qumran scrolls in this century has had a similar effect on the study of the NT, supplying, as it did, many details hitherto unknown about the Palestinian Jewish world in which John the Baptist and Jesus lived and about the Palestinian Jewish matrix from which early Christianity emerged.

The other area of investigation that contributed to the comparative study of religions was the ethnological study of the beliefs and practices of so-called primitive peoples. Highly influential in this area was the work of W. Schmidt,[152] not mentioned by the Commission, and of R. Otto,[153] who is mentioned.

As a result of all this investigation, there emerged in the early part of this century the *Religionsgeschichtliche Schule*. It sought to use the new evidence to explain the origin and development both of the ancient Israelite religion and of Christianity. Its effect on Christology is seen in its view of Jesus as a Palestinian Jew who lived in the Hellenistic world "fully imbued with syncretism and gnosticism" (1.1.4.3).

Though the Commission recognizes the validity of the comparative study of religions and its search for the "constant laws" operative in all religions, it expresses two cautions about this approach to Christology. First, it is reluctant to agree that Christianity is merely a fusion or a syncretism of elements from Judaism and contemporary pagan religions. This is seen as an oversimplification because Judaism itself a few centuries earlier had already come to grips with the influx of Hellenistic culture and religious thought, either by rejection or adoption. Indeed, it was mainly the *Greek* form of the OT that early Christianity took over from Judaism and made its own. Second, the Commission cautions against the idea that early Christian communities fabricated their beliefs and traditions out of whole cloth, as if they had no connection with a historical person and lacked all historical basis. Underlying this reaction is the recognition of a tendency in this approach to level out religions and deform them somewhat; the Commission is concerned to safeguard the "specific

---

[152]*Der Ursprung der Gottesidee: Eine historisch-kritische und positive Studie* (Münster: Aschendorff, 1912–36); cf. Albright, *From the Stone Age* 168–78.

[153]*The Idea of the Holy: An Inquiry into the Non-Rational Factor in the Idea of the Divine and Its Relation to the Rational* (6th ed.; London: Oxford University, 1931; repr., 1971).

character of the religion of Christ, linked to the newness of the gospel" (1.2.4.2).

In speaking of "some historians" who have even considered Christ to be no more than a "myth" (ibid.), the Commission names no one. But one readily thinks of B. Bauer, for whom not only Jesus but even Paul was a nonhistorical character of literary fiction, the product of some early Christian thinker's imagination.[154] Although such an extreme view is usually avoided by historians of religion, there are some who do regard Christianity as a mere syncretism, in which the "savior" of the Jewish tradition has become the "hero" of a religion of salvation in the manner of the Hellenistic mystery religions.

APPROACH 5:
THE APPROACH TO JESUS FROM JUDAISM

From the generic approach to Christology associated with the History of Religions School the Commission moves to the obviously specific religion that did affect Christology, viz. Judaism. For Jesus of Nazareth was a first-century Palestinian Jew, and "the Gospels depict him as one deeply rooted in his own land and in the tradition of his people" (1.1.5.1). Because of this, many Christian and Jewish scholars have devoted studies to what is known about him against such a background. Among Christian scholars the Commission mentions H. L. Strack and P. Billerbeck,[155] J. Bonsirven,[156] R. Le Déaut,[157] and M. McNamara.[158] Among Jewish scholars the Commission singles out J.

---

[154]*Kritik der evangelischen Geschichte des Johannes* (Bremen: Schünemann, 1840); *Kritik der evangelischen Geschichte der Synoptiker* (3 vols.; Leipzig: O. Wigand, 1841–42); *Kritik der paulinischen Briefe* (3 parts; Berlin: G. Hempel, 1850–52).

[155]*Kommentar zum Neuen Testament aus Talmud und Midrasch* (6 vols.; Munich: Beck, 1926–61).

[156]*Textes rabbiniques des deux premiers siècles chrétiens pour servir à l'intelligence du Nouveau Testament* (Rome: Biblical Institute, 1955).

[157]*The Message of the New Testament and the Aramaic Bible (Targum)* (Subsidia biblica 5; Rome: Biblical Institute, 1982), a revised form of *Liturgie juive et Nouveau Testament* (Rome: Biblical Institute, 1965).

[158]*Targum and Testament: Aramaic Paraphrases of the Hebrew Bible: A Light on the New Testament* (Shannon: Irish University, 1972).

Klausner,[159] M. Buber,[160] J. G. Montefiore,[161] P. Lapide,[162] Y. Yadin,[163] S. ben Chorin,[164] D. Flusser,[165] G. Vermes,[166] S. Sandmel.[167] It further mentions even the agnostic J. M. Allegro.[168] The studies of all these scholars have in one way or another emphasized "the Jewishness of Jesus" (1.1.5.2), the closeness of his teaching to that of Jewish teachers of his day, his relation to the temple and the synagogue. Some have even spoken of him as "brother Jesus," or as a teacher similar to the Pharisees, or have even compared his passion and death with the Isaian Suffering Servant (M. Buber). The Commission recognizes such studies as "a preliminary and necessary condition for the full understanding of his personality" and his role in the Father's plan of salvation (1.1.5.4; 1.2.5).

However, the Commission points out that the full understanding of Jesus cannot be conducted solely along such lines; it runs the risk of mutilating his personality if one merely insists that he was a Jew, a prophet, or a wonder-worker, only one of many Palestinian teachers—even perhaps the one most faithful to the Law and the Prophets. Moreover, even if one has to admit that the evangelists have sharpened the picture of his disputes with Pharisees and Scribes, the disputes were already real in his earthly lifetime. The movement that started with Jesus of Nazareth stems in part from "a new way of understanding one's relation to God and 'the fulfilment of Scripture,' which Jesus had brought to the people of his time through the gospel of the kingdom" (1.2.5.2). In other words, the better studies of Jesus' Jewish character cannot concentrate only on the

---

[159]*Jesus of Nazareth: His Life, Times, and Teaching* (New York: Macmillan, 1925).

[160]*Two Types of Faith* (London: Routledge & Kegan Paul, 1951) 102–13, esp. 105.

[161]*Rabbinic Literature and Gospel Teachings* (London: Macmillan, 1930; repr., New York: Ktav, 1970); *The Synoptic Gospels* (3 vols.; London: Macmillan, 1909).

[162]*The Resurrection of Jesus: A Jewish Perspective* (Minneapolis: Augsburg, 1983).

[163]*The Message of the Scrolls* (London: Weidenfeld and Nicolson, 1957) 186–88.

[164]*Bruder Jesus: Der Nazarener in jüdischer Sicht* (3rd ed.; Munich: DTV, 1970).

[165]*Jesus in Selbstzeugnissen und Bilddokumenten* (Reinbek bei Hamburg: Rohwalt, 1968); *Die rabbinischen Gleichnisse und der Gleichniserzähler Jesus* (Judaica et christiana 4; Bern: P. Lang, 1981).

[166]*Jesus the Jew: A Historian's Reading of the Gospels* (London: Collins, 1973); *Jesus and the World of Judaism* (Philadelphia: Fortress, 1983).

[167]*We Jews and Jesus* (New York: Oxford University, 1965).

[168]*The Sacred Mushroom and the Cross* (Garden City, N.Y.: Doubleday, 1970); *The Dead Sea Scrolls and the Christian Myth* (Newton Abbott: Westbridge, 1979; Buffalo, N.Y.: Prometheus, 1984).

similarities but must also admit the differences and the disagreements. For he was not only a famous first-century Palestinian Jewish individual; he was more.

APPROACH 6:
CHRISTOLOGY AND SALVATION HISTORY

One of the reactions to the "Life of Jesus Research" in the 19th century was to substitute for the secular view of history implied in it a religious interpretation of human history. Such a reaction is traced back to J. T. Beck and J. C. K. von Hofmann,[169] who adopted the idea of *Heilsgeschichte*, "salvation history." According to this view, one judges human affairs in the light of the gospel, and meaningful events are actually found in them that are regarded as traces of God's intervention in those affairs, and that reveal God Himself as directing the course of human history toward a goal. Indeed, such events "make up the very texture of Scripture itself" (1.1.6.1). Moreover, the direction of it toward such a goal or consummation invests it with a distinctively eschatological aspect. Under such a heading, then, the Commission classifies two slightly differing Christological approaches: (1) an approach to Christology that concentrates on the titles given to Jesus in the NT, and (2) an approach that has a pronounced eschatological cast.

Some modern scholars have concentrated on the titles of Christ; thus V. Taylor,[170] F. Hahn,[171] L. Sabourin,[172] A. Feuillet,[173] or P. Benoit.[174] But it is above all the writings of O. Cullmann that the Commission has in mind, and these are the reason why title Christology is discussed under salvation history. Cullmann not only worked out an attempt "to depict the centre of the New Testament in a salvation-histor-

---

[169]See E.-W. Wendebourg, "Die heilsgeschichtliche Theologie J. Chr. v. Hofmanns in ihrem Verhältnis zur romantischen Weltanschauung," *ZTK* 52 (1955) 64–104.

[170]*The Names of Jesus* (New York: St. Martin's, 1953).

[171]*The Titles of Jesus in Christology: Their History in Early Christianity* (London: Lutterworth, 1969).

[172]*Les noms et les titres de Jésus* (Bruges: Desclée de Brouwer, 1963).

[173]*Le Christ, sagesse de Dieu, d'après les épîtres pauliniennes* (EBib; Paris: Gabalda, 1966).

[174]"The Divinity of Christ in the Synoptic Gospels," *Son and Saviour*, ed. A. Gelin (Baltimore: Helicon, 1960) 57–92.

ical theology,"[175] but he also authored an important study, *Christology of the New Testament*,[176] which was mainly devoted to the titles of Christ and made use of the distinction between "functional Christology" and "ontological Christology" (1.1.6.2a). This distinction is seen as important because most of the NT titles for Christ refer to his soteriological role, i.e. his function in God's plan of salvation. This is seen to be true even of those that hint at his relation to the Father, for most of the titles say little about his internal constitution or metaphysical make-up. The soteriological emphasis thus given to Christology is welcome, because it, in effect, joins aspects that were traditionally treated separately in the classic tracts *De Verbo Incarnato* and *De Christo Redemptore*.

The Commission also brings under this heading of salvation-history Christology the approaches of two modern German theologians, that of the Lutheran W. Pannenberg[177] and that of the German Reformed J. Moltmann.[178] It recalls the eschatological aspect of Pannenberg's Christology, in referring to his view of Jesus' resurrection as an anticipation (*prolepsis*) of the end of all human history. Pannenberg thinks that the truth of this fact can be proved by historical investigation (*Historie*) and that in this way "the divinity of Jesus is demonstrated" (1.1.6.2b). Moltmann's eschatological perspective is even more pronounced: all human history appears to be polarized by a promise. Those who accept in faith such an orientation find in it the source of a hope of sharing in God's salvation, a hope that has an impact on all of human history (announced in the OT's prophetic promises and fulfilled in the death and resurrection of Jesus, the instrument of salvation). In such a Christology Moltmann works out many of its psychological, social, and political aspects. In these aspects the Commission sees his Christology not only involving soteriology but even leading to a program of action (1.1.6.2c).

It is a bit puzzling, however, to see the Commission relate to this

---

[175]*Salvation in History* (New York: Harper & Row, 1967) 11; see also his *Christ and Time* (rev. ed.; Philadelphia: Westminster, 1964).

[176]*Die Christologie des Neuen Testaments* (3rd ed.; Tübingen: Mohr [Siebeck], 1963); *The Christology of the New Testament* (rev. ed.; Philadelphia: Westminster, 1963).

[177]*Jesus—God and Man* (Philadelphia: Westminster, 1968) 53–190; see also *Revelation As History* (New York: Macmillan, 1968).

[178]*The Crucified God: The Cross of Christ As the Foundation of Christian Theology* (New York: Harper & Row, 1974); cf. *Theology of Hope: On the Ground and the Implications of Christian Eschatology* (New York: Harper & Row, 1967) 95–229.

Moltmannian emphasis a "similar concern" said to be found in some examples of "social exegesis" (ibid.).[179] No explanation is given of the connection between such exegesis and Christology or eschatology, or even with salvation history.

But the Commission rightly sees this salvation-history approach to Christology as related to the patristic and medieval teaching about the "*oikonomia* of salvation" (1.1.6.1), for it is presenting in a new form, expressed in fuller biblical terminology, what the patristic and medieval writers expressed as *oikonomia*, the Father's dispensation of salvation for the human race.[180]

There is, however, an obvious difficulty in this approach, and that is found in its use of the word "history." This word cannot have the same connotation when it is used of, say, Jesus of Nazareth as a figure in bygone "history," and of his role in "salvation history." The romance languages and English have only one word, "history," whereas German has two, *Historie/historisch* and *Geschichte/geschichtlich* (noun and adjective). Though the distinction between them is not always clear in German and they are often used interchangeably, at least since the time of M. Kähler (1896) German theologians have used them with different nuances. For them *Historie* means an account of the causal connections in human affairs, the subject matter of historical research that seeks to prescind from presuppositions or prejudices and to establish objectively what happened. But *Geschichte* means rather an account of the mutual encounter of human beings, including all that affects their personal existence and experience.[181] The Commission refers to this dis-

---

[179]See G. Theissen, *Sociology of Early Palestinian Christianity* (Philadelphia: Fortress, 1978); E. A. Judge, *The Social Pattern of the Christian Groups in the First Century* (London: Tyndale, 1960); A. J. Malherbe, *Social Aspects of Early Christianity: Rockwell Lectures* (Baton Rouge: Louisiana State University, 1977).

[180]This sense of *oikonomia* is undoubtedly derived from Eph 1:10; 3:9. It is further used in Ignatius, *Eph.* 18.2; 20.1; Clement of Alexandria, *Strom.* 1.19 §94,1 (GCS 52.60); Origen, *De princ.* 3.1,14 (GCS 22.220); Irenaeus, *Adv. haer.* 1.10,3 (SC 24.162); 4.33,7 (SC 100.819). For reasons why modern theologians prefer to speak of "salvation history" rather than the *oikonomia* of salvation, see O. Cullmann, *Salvation in History* 74–78.

[181]See M. Kähler, *The So-Called Historical Jesus and the Historic Biblical Christ*, ed. C. E. Braaten (Philadelphia: Fortress, 1964). For the Bultmannian-Schniewind usage, see J. Schniewind, "A Reply to Bultmann," *Kerygma and Myth: A Theological Debate*, ed. H. W. Bartsch (2 vols.; London: SPCK, 1960–62) 1.45–100, esp. 82. Cf. N. J. Young, *History and Existential Theology: The Role of History in the Thought of Rudolf Bultmann* (Philadelphia: Westminster, 1969) 22–26.

tinction between *der historische Jesus* and *Heilsgeschichte*. It has always been a problem to translate these German words (nouns and adjectives) into English and to preserve the nuances of the German. It is easier for the adjective than for the noun; *historisch* is usually rendered "historical," and *geschichtlich* is rendered "historic,"[182] whereas both nouns *Historie* and *Geschichte* are rendered as "history." The consequences of this distinction will have ramifications below in the discussion of Bultmann's approach, but at the moment the Commission contents itself with reiterating that the study of salvation history is not based merely on "empirical facts" or experience, access to which is gained "by the study of documents" (1.2.6.1), for it involves an "intelligence that comes from faith," even a decision of faith. In the long run, both "the historical Jesus" and "the historic Christ" are involved in salvation history.[183]

Noteworthy is what the Commission says in this paragraph about "the resurrection of Christ" (note, not the resurrection of Jesus!): "by its very nature it cannot be proved in any empirical way" (1.2.6.2), i.e. it is not the subject matter of *Historie* or accessible to a historian's scientific investigation. By the resurrection Jesus is introduced into "the world to come." Thus the Commission makes it clear that the resurrection of Christ was not a mere resuscitation or a return to earthly life. The reality of the resurrection, however, can be deduced "from the appearances of Christ in glory to certain preordained witnesses" (ibid.) and corroborated by the fact of the empty tomb. It is known to the believer's "open heart" or "decision of faith." In making this distinction the Commission is siding more with Kähler and Bultmann than with Pannenberg, who sought to transcend the dichotomy between *Historie* and *Geschichte*.[184]

---

[182]So by C. E. Braaten in *The So-Called Historical Jesus* (see n. 181) 20–23.

[183]It is also important to recall here a distinction that the Commission does not make: between "the earthly Jesus of past history" and "the historical Jesus" (*der historische Jesus*), because the latter is in reality the designation of Jesus of Nazareth as the subject matter of historical research—what the historical method can reconstruct about his earthly existence by means of documents, monuments, etc. This reconstructed "historical Jesus" clearly has validity, but it may not correspond 100 percent with "the earthly Jesus" who walked the roads of ancient Palestine.

[184]Recall the summary of Pannenberg's position given in 1.1.6.2b. Involved here are Pannenberg's ideas on analogy and the right way of speaking about such things as the resurrection, and even of God. See E. A. Johnson, "The Right Way To Speak about God? Pannenberg on Analogy," *TS* 43 (1982) 673–92.

As for the titles of Christ, the Commission not only notes the distinction between those that may stem from use by the earthly Jesus himself (with no examples given) and those born of confessional affirmations formulated by "theologians of the apostolic age." But it considers as more important the distinction between functional titles (i.e. those descriptive of his salvific role) and relational titles (i.e. those descriptive of his relation to God). In this case it mentions two, Word and Son, but nothing is said about the origin of them. However, title Christology is viewed as an incomplete Christology because little account is taken of Jesus' deeds, conduct, or habits, which in the long run would reveal more than the titles "what is most profound about a person" (1.2.6.3).

The Commission further recognizes the validity of the eschatological dimension of salvation-history Christology and the consequences it has for Christian life and activity. But it calls attention to the ambiguity in the term "eschatological," noting the lack of clarity with which modern interpreters of Jesus' words surround them (1.2.6.4). Noteworthy here is the lack of any suggestion for a proper understanding of the "eschatological" problem of NT texts. The Commission contents itself with asking four rhetorical questions that have continually vexed NT interpreters and skirts the problem itself with the sole comment that "a Christology true to its colors ought to explain all questions of this sort" (ibid.). Amen! But who can answer them? Not even the Biblical Commission has tried.

APPROACH 7:
CHRISTOLOGY AND ANTHROPOLOGY

The Commission groups under this title various methodologies that it considers to have a common starting point in "different aspects of human experience or of anthropology" (1.1.7), using "anthropology" in a theological, not a sociological, sense. After relating, with little precise explanation, this approach to older problems in apologetics (e.g. the use of "signs of credibility," or the Modernist appeal to general religious experience, or even the Blondelian intrinsic analysis of human action), the Commission moves on to four examples of Christologies of this anthropological sort.

Synopsis of Teilhard

The first is that of P. Teilhard de Chardin, who, in making a synthesis of theology and modern science, regarded the universe as an evolutionary process that is ever moving toward systems of greater complexity and higher levels of consciousness. The process has had certain critical moments or thresholds, when new levels were reached by "leaps." The entire process is moving toward an omega point, when all things will be caught up or recapitulated in Christ. "The final branch/ shoot" (*le bourgeon terminal*) of the evolutionary process is humanity itself, or the human phenomenon, which also takes part in the direction of the process. But it has now a sacramental character because it has been "Christified," as a consequence of the "leap" of the Incarnation. Jesus Christ, the incarnate Son of God, is thus the unifying principle of human history, and, indeed, of the entire universe itself. Through his birth and resurrection the meaning of the "human phenomenon" is disclosed to those who believe (1.1.7.1).[185]

In assessing the Christology that is part of Teilhard de Chardin's view of the universe and the human phenomenon, the Commission contents itself with asking two rhetorical questions that, in effect, merely repeat standard criticisms of his views: his Christology is too abstract, ideal, even idyllic, since it seems to leave little room for the concrete picture of Jesus of Nazareth and his founding of the Church in a "Jewish milieu," or for the historical dimension of Jesus' death on the cross and his relation to that cross. Again, the orientation of everything toward the omega point is optimistic. It does not seem to cope sufficiently with evil in the world and in human beings or with the redemptive aspect of Jesus' life, death, and resurrection (1.2.7.1). The Commission thus finds his Christology deficient, in need of complementary studies of the person of Jesus and of the variety of NT Christologies.[186]

---

[185]*The Phenomenon of Man* (New York: Harper, 1959); *Man's Place in Nature: The Human Zoological Group* (London: Collins, 1966); *The Divine Milieu* (New York: Harper, 1960). Cf. C. F. Mooney, *Teilhard de Chardin and the Mystery of Christ* (New York: Harper & Row, 1966); T. M. King, "The Milieux Teilhard Left Behind," *America* 152 (1985) 249–53.

[186]Some of this criticism was leveled against Teilhard de Chardin even in his lifetime, and some footnotes in *The Phenomenon of Man* reveal how he was trying to cope with it. Cf. R. L. Faricy, "Teilhard de Chardin's Theology of Redemption," *TS* 27 (1966) 553–79. Strangely enough, the Commission is silent about a significant aspect of Teilhard's Christology, his views about three natures in Christ: "cette troisième 'nature' du Christ

Second, the Christology of K. Rahner is more properly classed as
an anthropological Christology (1.1.7.2)[187] because, even if Rahner is
careful to preserve traditional teaching about the hypostatic union and
the two natures in Christ, his real starting point is *anthrōpos*, "human
being," whence all his other ideas or thought-categories flow. Ontology,
cosmology, even theology have to begin from an *anthropo-logy*. A human being exists only as one of many individuals linked together by mutual relations of interdependence. For Rahner, a human being is not just
a rational animal (in the Aristotelian sense) but a "spirit in the world,"
because of a yearning for the infinite, as a being oriented toward the incomprehensible Godhead. Beginning with the experience of human
beings, Rahner appeals to the transcendental aspects of that experience:
freedom, love, hope, the desire to know, and choice. Through these aspects of existence a human being comes to experience and know God,
even if in an unthematized way. Moreover, these aspects of human experience find their full expression in Christ, so that anthropology may
be understood as deficient Christology, and Christology as the fulfilment
of anthropology. Rahner's Christology is anthropological because there
would be no Christology unless there had been a Christ in *human* existence and history. The concrete history that is named Jesus had an inner
relatedness to the original, primary, i.e. transcendental constitution of
humanity. In his early career Rahner centered more on the Incarnation,
in which humanity finds the fulfilment of its yearning for the infinite.
Later on he gave more attention (than he had before) to the death and

---

(nature ni humaine, ni divine, mais 'cosmique')." See *The Heart of Matter* (London: Collins, 1978) 93; *Toward the Future* (London: Collins, 1975) 198. Cf. H. de Lubac, *Teilhard
de Chardin: The Man and His Meaning* (New York: Hawthorn Books, 1965) 40; King,
"The Milieux" 250.

[187]*Foundations of Christian Faith: An Introduction to the Idea of Christianity* (New
York: Seabury, 1978); "Current Problems in Christology," *Theological Investigations* 1
(London: Darton, Longmans & Todd, 1961) 149–200; "On the Theology of the Incarnation," ibid. 4 (1966) 105–20; "The Position of Christology in the Church between Exegesis and Dogmatics," ibid. 11 (1974) 185–214; "Christology in the Setting of Modern
Man's Understanding of Himself and of His World," ibid. 215–29; "The Death of Jesus
and the Closure of Revelation," ibid. 18 (1983) 132–42; "What Does It Mean Today To
Believe in Jesus Christ?" ibid. 143–56; "Jesus Christ: IV. History of Dogma and Theology," *Sacramentum mundi* (6 vols.; New York: Herder and Herder, 1968–70) 3. 192–
209. Cf. K. Rahner and W. Thüsing, *Christologie—Systematisch und exegetisch: Arbeits-
grundlagen für eine interdisziplinäre Vorlesung* (QD 55; Freiburg im B.: Herder, 1972)
15–78.

resurrection of Jesus and to a Christian's share in them. Christ is the center of salvation history, for in him the transcendental aspects of human experience find full realization. As the Word is the real, symbolic expression of the Father within the Trinity, so the human nature in Christ is the real, symbolic expression of the divine Word in time and space. As a result, Christ's resurrection, his continued life in the Church, and the gift of faith granted in the Spirit to believers bring it about that the goal of humanity is realized in a new and otherwise unattainable way. Rahner's view thus includes both an earlier emphasis on a Christology "from above," centering on the divine Word's assuming of human flesh, and a later development of a Christology "from below," centering on the human life of Jesus moving toward the cross and God's ultimate faithfulness in the resurrection.

In assessing Rahner's Christology, the Commission merely notes that it may not find acceptance among those who would not grant its philosophical premises and that it does not reckon sufficiently with the variety or multiplicity of Christologies within the NT itself (1.2.7.2).

Third, from a different viewpoint, H. Küng's Christology is also considered anthropological because he "concentrates his study on the historical existence of the Jew that was Jesus" (1.1.7.3).[188] Indeed, Küng finds fault with various current conceptions of Jesus Christ (the Christ of piety, the Christ of dogma, the Christ of the enthusiasts, the Christ of literature, and even the Christ of myth [e.g. J. M. Allegro]) and draws from the NT documents (considered by him as "committed testimonies") his picture of the "real Christ," a picture of the preresurrection Jesus, "a Jewish human being, a genuine Jew."[189] The 20th-century Christian, faced with materialism, secularity, technocracy, and increasing contact with other world religions, and looking for what is distinctive in Christianity, must adopt the attitude of the first disciples. Such a Christian must begin the analysis with "the real human Jesus, his historical message and manifestation, his life and fate, his historical reality and historical activity, and then ask about the relationship of this human being Jesus to God, about his unity with the Father." This Küng calls "a historical Christology 'from below,' in the light of the concrete

---

[188]*On Being a Christian* (Garden City, N.Y.: Doubleday, 1976) 145–58.
[189]Ibid. 166.

Jesus.''[190] This Jesus espoused the cause of God (His will, the kingdom and its message) and of humanity (solidarity with human beings and action on behalf of people, even of enemies). This commitment to God and humanity brought him to his death. For Küng, Jesus' resurrection is an intervention of God involving ''a completely new mode of existence in God's wholly different mode of existence.''[191] But, more important, it is God's confirmation and vindication of Jesus' life and death. The mode of life initiated and promoted by the preresurrection Jesus does not cease to flow in the Church, thanks to the Holy Spirit. The Church is ''the community of those who have become involved in the case of Jesus Christ and who witness to it as hope for all men.''[192] As a result, Küng sees Christian conduct as a ''radical humanism'' with social relevance that gives people real freedom (in the legal order, in the struggle for power), a freedom from the pressure of consumption, and a freedom to serve others. This is human existence transfigured by Christ.

In assessing Küng's Christology, the Commission acknowledges as valid his point of departure in considering Jesus as a true human being (and all that Küng spells out under that heading). But it finds that ''doctrinal elements amassed in this way depend too much on the critical hypotheses employed at the outset'' (1.2.7.3). For Küng's tendency is to regard the older, earlier NT writers as closer to the ''historical Jesus.'' He is reluctant to accept the later, more explicit testimony of other NT writers.[193] Likewise, the Commission criticizes Küng's reluctance to use the NT data about Jesus that have been joined with reflection on him and on his relation to the OT, ''the authority of which neither Jesus nor his disciples ever called in question.'' Hence Küng's interpretation of the NT itself ''may turn out to be erroneous'' (ibid.). What is deficient in his approach is not the emphasis on the preresurrection Christ—indeed, Küng's stress on Jesus' humanity is welcome—but the neglect of the NT data that depend on the postresurrection experience of the early Church recorded in the same documents. His is a selective reading of the NT.

---

[190]Ibid. 133. Küng relies heavily on the historical-critical method of interpreting the NT, convinced that ''only faith and knowledge combined—a faith that knows and a knowledge that believes—are capable today of understanding the true Christ in his breadth and depth'' (166).

[191]Ibid. 350: ''Resurrection means dying into God'' (359).

[192]Ibid. 478.

[193]Ibid. 151–53, 450.

Küng does discuss the Johannine "Word of God" and considers him as the manifestation of God in the work and person of Jesus;[194] he also emphasizes that the Johannine prologue "culminates in 'and the Word was made flesh.' "[195] But he seems to avoid discussing "and the Word was God" (Jn 1:1) or Thomas' acclamation, "My Lord and my God" (20:28). These are affirmations within a major NT Christology and cannot be excluded from consideration.

Fourth, still another anthropological Christology is that of E. Schillebeeckx (1.1.7.4).[196] Realizing that traditional Christology since Nicaea has been dominated by the Johannine data, Schillebeeckx bases his "experiment in Christology" on the Synoptic data, thus preferring a Christology "from below," rooted in Mark and "Q" and dependent on the new quest for the historical Jesus of the Post-Bultmannians. His concern has been to give serious consideration, as a Christian theologian, to the results of the modern study of Scripture. Though "belief in Jesus as the 'final saving good' is to be justified only in faith," it is also subject to "the exigencies of critical rationality."[197]

Schillebeeckx is aware of the many difficulties associated with earlier critical attempts to construct a Christology either on the "diverse Christologies" of the NT, or on an alleged, but very subjective, "gospel within the Gospels," or on a supposed "single 'primitive kerygma,' " or on the "diverse 'oldest pictures of Jesus,' " or on "Jesus' own self-awareness" (about which "we know very little"), or on his *ipsissima verba et facta,* or even on the "credal statements and homologues in the Bible."[198] Hence he rather makes his starting point "a historical and critical approach, set within an intention of faith." This he finds within "the Christian movement itself": a "oneness of experience" unified by "its pointing to the one figure of Jesus," even if pluriform in its verbal expression.[199] This one, collective, community experience obliged people in Jesus' day to define the ultimate meaning of life by reference to him. This was the process by which Christian belief came into being;

---

[194]Ibid. 444.

[195]Ibid. 446.

[196]*Jesus: An Experiment in Christology* (New York: Seabury, 1979). Cf. *Christ: The Experience of Jesus As Lord* (New York: Crossroad, 1981).

[197]*Jesus* 32.

[198]Ibid. 52–55.

[199]Ibid. 56.

through this movement early Christians experienced the Spirit in the remembrance of Jesus: *pneuma* and *anamnesis*. The criterion for the Christian Church's preaching of Jesus was not accessibility to him in se, but only through the experience of his immediate disciples before and after his death. ". . . Christian faith entails not only the personal living presence of the glorified Jesus, but also a link with his life on earth, for it is precisely that life that has been acknowledged and empowered by God through the Resurrection."[200] Early Christians affirmed the identity of the earthly Jesus and the risen Christ, and their experience of both becomes normative for all who are Christians. Thus historical criteria do not guarantee Christian faith, but they can show that "framed within the acknowledgement of salvation imparted by God in Jesus Christ, the gospels should be seen as an accurate reflex of Jesus of Nazareth."[201] In reading the NT in this way, Schillebeeckx concentrates on the identification of Jesus as "the eschatological prophet" during his earthly ministry and on his "abba experience." Jesus' insistence on these aspects of his life led eventually to his being condemned as a false teacher; and his defiance of the high priest (see Deut 17:12) led to his death. The *identification* of Jesus was thus already under way before the resurrection. Yet the preresurrection eschatological prophet came to be interpreted subsequently as the Christ, Son of God, Lord,[202] so that the distinction of the historical Jesus and the Christ of faith is to be rejected, or at least reversed. For Schillebeeckx, the resurrection is the divine vindication of Jesus' life; the same people who knew him as the eschatological prophet recognized in the risen Christ the victor over death, who is thus the pledge of salvation for all who become part of his movement.

The Commission rightly recognizes the legitimacy of Schillebeeckx' insistence on the continuity of the experience of Jesus' immediate followers both before and after his resurrection. But it suspects, as it did in the case of Küng, that his initial hypotheses are too restricted (based on the Synoptics, or rather on Mark and "Q"). Moreover, the path from the identification of Jesus as the eschatological prophet (during his earthly ministry) to the faith identification of him as the Son of God etc. is insufficiently explained (see further 1.2.7.4).

---

[200]Ibid. 76.
[201]Ibid. 90.
[202]Ibid. 440.

APPROACH 8:
THE EXISTENTIALIST INTERPRETATION
OF JESUS CHRIST

After the discussion of four anthropological Christologies, the Commission moves on to the existentialist approach of R. Bultmann. Whereas only one paragraph had been devoted to the description of the approach of Teilhard de Chardin, Rahner, Küng, and Schillebeeckx, four are now devoted to Bultmann's approach. This is not only because his contribution to the study of Christology has been more biblical, but also because he has so profoundly influenced the thinking of so many modern Christian exegetes and theologians.[203]

Bultmann's starting points were the impasse of the Life of Jesus Research (see 1.1.3.1) and the idea of the History of Religions School that Christianity was a syncretism (1.1.4.3). Borrowing from Kähler the distinction of "the Jesus of history" and "the Christ of faith" (see 1.2.6.1), Bultmann refined it with his existentialist interpretation.[204] With little interest in the Jesus of history, save to affirm a vague connection between the obedient way Jesus acted in his relation to God and the eventual gospel "kerygma," Bultmann reduced the latter to "the proclamation of forgiveness extended by God to sinners" (1.1.8.2). Or, to let Bultmann speak for himself:

> Christian faith did not exist until there was a Christian kerygma, i.e., a kerygma proclaiming Jesus Christ—specifically Jesus Christ the Crucified and Risen One—to be God's eschatological act of salvation. He was first so proclaimed in the kerygma of the earliest Church, *not in the message of the historical Jesus,* even though that Church frequently introduced

---

[203]See his *Primitive Christianity in Its Contemporary Setting* (London: Thames and Hudson, 1956); *Theology of the New Testament* (2 vols.; London: SCM, 1952–55); *Jesus and the Word* (New York: Scribner's, 1935); *Faith and Understanding* 1 (New York: Harper & Row, 1969); *Jesus Christ and Mythology* (New York: Scribner's, 1958). Cf. *Kerygma und Mythos* (6 vols.; ed. H. W. Bartsch et al.; Hamburg/Volksdorf: H. Reich, 1948–75 [the first two volumes have been translated; see n. 181 above]).

[204]See his "New Testament and Mythology," *Kerygma and Myth,* 1.1–44; cf. J. Schniewind, "A Reply to Bultmann," 82–87; and Bultmann's answer, 117–18.

into its account of Jesus' message motifs of its own proclamation. Thus, theological thinking—the theology of the New
Testament—begins with the *kerygma* of the earliest Church
and not before.[205]

What little of "Jesus' message" is retained by Bultmann in his idea
of the Christian kerygma is reduced to this: his eschatological message
of the kingdom of God and its immediately impending irruption, now
already making itself felt. Jesus stood in the historical context of Jewish
expectations about the world's end and God's new future, the sign of
which was Jesus' own person, as he called for decision (i.e. obedience
to the will of God). As a formulation of God's demand made of humanity, it was a protest against Jewish legalism (recall the antitheses of the
Sermon on the Mount). God's will was a demand for love, in which Jesus' eschatological message and his ethical message constitute a unity.
"This message is signified by the cross of Jesus, which is the genuine
'word' of God inscribed in a historical fact" (1.1.8.2).[206] "The cross
and the resurrection form a single, indivisible cosmic event"[207] that
brings judgment to the world and opens for human beings the possibility
of authentic life or existence. But the resurrection is an article of faith,
proclaimed together with the cross and its saving efficacy, the eschatological event, proclaimed in the kerygma. In this Christian kerygma
the proclaimer became the proclaimed, announced as the Messiah and
(coming) Son of Man. As such, he was still the proclaimer of
God's radical demand, and the decision of faith becomes the existential response to that demand and the means of a new, fully authentic
Christian existence.

In 1.1.8.3, the Commission recalls Bultmann's demythologization
of the three-storied world of the NT, supernatural forces, miracles, etc.,
and his assertion that an existentialist interpretation is the only solution
whereby the truth of the kerygma can be recovered for those who do not
think in mythological terms. The Commission further acknowledges
Bultmann's contribution to the form-critical study of the Gospels, es-

---

[205]*Theology* 1.3; emphasis added.
[206]Cf. "New Testament and Mythology," *Kerygma and Myth,* 1.1–44, esp. 35–38.
[207]Ibid. 38.

pecially his emphasis on the *Sitz im Leben* or life-setting in the early Church, which gave "form" to so many units of the gospel tradition.[208]

Bultmann's ideas have long since been assessed by many writers of different backgrounds and confessions, and the Commission limits its assessment of them to eight main points, after frankly acknowledging his great positive contribution to the relation of biblical exegesis, theological study, and living Christian faith. The risks in Bultmann's approach to Christology are seen in the following points: (1) In considering the historical Jesus as of minimal importance for Christian faith, Bultmann excludes Jesus and his message (both eschatological and ethical) as the origin of Christology, or at least reduces them to insignificance. (2) In this attitude to Jesus, who lived out the demands of the Mosaic Torah, Bultmann has reduced the relation of Christology and of Christianity itself to the OT almost to nothing (1.2.8.1). (3) Bultmann's demythologization becomes excessive in that it reduces the symbolic language (often derived from the OT) to mere mythological language. (4) The existentialist interpretation of the NT, coupled with that demythologization, runs the risk of reducing Christology to an "anthropology"—not that it makes Bultmann's approach to Christology in any way similar to the anthropological Christologies discussed above, but that it substitutes, in effect, an "anthropology," a doctrine about human beings and their existence before God, for Christology, which should be a teaching about Jesus Christ and his meaning for humanity. (5) The Commission finds no little difficulty in Bultmann's analysis of the relation of what he sometimes calls "the miracle of the resurrection"[209] to the "past historical event which is the crucifixion of Jesus."[210] For if the resurrection is miraculous, then it becomes for Bultmann mythological, and it is not clear how the resurrection and the cross are to be related. (6) The Commission similarly finds difficulty with Bultmann's view that "Son of God" was merely a mythological title stem-

---

[208]As does the Commission, I must limit myself here to the consideration of Bultmann's Christology; it is impossible to discuss further ramifications of his theology. For a good introduction to the latter, see G. Bornkamm, "The Theology of Rudolf Bultmann," in *The Theology of Rudolf Bultmann*, ed. C. W. Kegle (New York: Harper & Row, 1966) 3–20 (with a reply by Bultmann himself, 257–58; and an extensive bibliography up to 1965, 289–310).

[209]"New Testament and Mythology" 38–39.

[210]Ibid. 41. Cf. "The Christology of the New Testament," *Faith and Understanding* 1.202–85.

ming from "the later Hellenistic Church"[211] and one not used of Jesus by NT writers "in a unique sense" (1.2.8.3). If Bultmann is right, then why did God address his last word, his "eschatological word," to us in him "through the medium of the cross"? (7) The Commission ultimately sees Bultmann's position reduced to a form of fideism, because his reaction to "proofs" or "signs" stems from his own view of natural theology.[212] (8) Bultmann's radical demand for a "decision of faith" loosely linked with "the demand for love"[213] is seen to have little room for "the positive demands of justice" (1.2.8.4). The last two criticisms have to do more with Bultmann's theology than with his Christology.

Twice (1.1.8.4; 1.2.8.4) the Commission notes that disciples and followers of Bultmann, though they have not rejected his principal studies or the global aim of his interpretation, have seen the need to trace the origin of Christology back to Jesus himself, i.e. not just to his "eschatological message." In the first instance, reference is made explicitly to E. Käsemann.[214] This is an allusion to the so-called New Quest for the Historical Jesus, an overdue sophisticated approach to Christology that tries to avoid Scylla and Charybdis, the extremes of Bultmann's skepticism and the impasse of the Life of Jesus Research.

APPROACH 9:
CHRISTOLOGY AND SOCIAL CONCERNS

A different approach to Christology has emerged among students of the NT, theologians, and others, who look to these writings for what

---

[211]The titles "Son of God" and "Son of the Most High" have recently been discovered in a Qumran Aramaic text from Palestine, which has not yet been fully published. I have already discussed the pertinence of this evidence to the problem of the so-called Hellenistic provenience of the title "Son of God" in "The Contribution of Qumran Aramaic to the Study of the New Testament," *A Wandering Aramean: Collected Aramaic Essays* (SBLMS 25; Missoula, Mont.: Scholars, 1979) 85–113, esp. 90–94.

[212]See "The Problem of 'Natural Theology,' " *Faith and Understanding* 1.313–31.
[213]*Theology* 1.18–19.

[214]"The Problem of the Historical Jesus," *Essays on New Testament Themes* (SBT 41; London: SCM, 1964) 15–47. Cf. N A. Dahl, "The Problem of the Historical Jesus," *Kerygma and History: A Symposium on the Theology of Rudolf Bultmann*, ed. C. Braaten and R. A. Harrisville (Nashville: Abingdon, 1962) 138–71; J. M. Robinson, *A New Quest for the Historical Jesus* (SBT 25; Naperville, Ill.: Allenson, 1959); N. Perrin, *Rediscovering the Teaching of Jesus* (New York: Harper & Row, 1967).

they may contribute to a renewal of life in human society. This society is not without its modern, contemporary ills and injustices, and some of these students are of the opinion that Jesus' "praxis" may shed some light on such social problems. This approach can be traced back to the "Utopian" Socialists of the 19th century, e.g. people like P.-J. Proudhon.[215] K. Marx is even singled out by the Commission as one who, though he regarded religion as "the opium of the people," was at least indirectly influenced by biblical messianism (1.1.9.1), and F. Engels, an advocate of "class struggle," is said to have appealed to the principle of hope found in the Book of Revelation.

Related to such thinking is the modern approach to Christology employed in various forms of liberation theology that depict Jesus as "Christ the Liberator" (1.1.9.2). This approach presents Jesus as one who espoused the cause of the poor and reacted against the abusive oppression of his contemporaries by authorities in economic, political, ideological, and even religious spheres of life. Here the Commission mentions the influence of S. G. F. Brandon, who depicted Jesus as a political opponent of the Roman occupation of Palestine.[216] The Commission recognizes that some forms of liberation theology are more radical than others, singling out the approaches of G. Gutiérrez[217] and L. Boff[218] with their ideas of liberation that embrace "all human affairs" (1.1.9.2), whereas that of J. Sobrino[219] is more limited to social relations.

Strikingly enough, the Commission does not group these liberation theologians with proponents of Marxism who have made appeal to Jesus' "praxis." It groups them separately (1.1.9.3), because the liberation theologians write as Christians, even if they have been inspired by Marx-

---

[215]*Oeuvres complètes de P.-J. Proudhon: Nouvelle édition*, ed. C. Bouglé and H. Moysset (4 vols.; Paris: Librairie des sciences politiques et sociales, 1936–38). Cf. H. de Lubac, *The Un-Marxian Socialist: A Study of Proudhon* (New York: Sheed & Ward, 1948).

[216]*Jesus and the Zealots: A Study of the Political Factor in Primitive Christianity* (New York: Scribner's, 1967) 322–58.

[217]*A Theology of Liberation: History, Politics and Salvation* (Maryknoll, N.Y.: Orbis, 1973).

[218]*Jesus Christ Liberator: A Critical Christology for Our Time* (Maryknoll, N.Y.: Orbis, 1978).

[219]*Christology at the Crossroads: A Latin American Approach* (Maryknoll, N.Y.: Orbis, 1978).

ist teaching or analysis. However, E. Bloch[220] and M. Machoveč[221] are recognized by the Commission as atheists who nonetheless appeal to the NT idea of hope or to Jesus' "praxis" as a form of brotherly love that may be used as a guide for a new form of human society, or even of an "integral communism." From a slightly different perspective, some students of the Gospels, inspired by the Marxist analysis of human and social affairs, have subjected them to a materialist interpretation, i.e. one free of an "ecclesiastical ideology," e.g. F. Belo,[222] without, however, adopting all aspects of "dialectical materialism" (1.1.9.4).

Strangely enough, the Commission relates to these approaches to Christology, born of social concerns, that of J. B. Metz, adding, indeed, "from a notably different point of view" (1.1.9.6). Though Metz's Christology is a form of "practical theology," concerned about oppression, social justice, and the liberation of human beings, it differs considerably from those that are more Marxist-oriented.[223]

While admitting that liberation theology rightly stresses that Christ's salvation is not to be understood solely in a "spiritual" sense, but is meant to free from all oppressive tyranny, the Commission feels that risky consequences can be drawn from such a generic redemptive view, unless it is joined with ethical demands consonant with the precepts of the NT itself. The Commission further criticizes the Marxist and materialist interpretations of Jesus and his gospel in that they are too closely linked with their own philosophical, sociological, and anthropological presuppositions, which run the risk of falsifying the nature of God, of Christ, and even of humanity itself (1.2.9.1 and 2 end).

In its description (1.1.9.5) the Commission had noted the tendency of the liberation-theology approaches to concentrate on the Jesus of history and his "praxis" (even linking with this view teaching that has been traditionally regarded as soteriology or social ethics). But it goes further (1.2.9.2) in criticizing the arbitrary mode of reading the NT that partly

[220]*Das Prinzip Hoffnung: In fünf Teilen* (Frankfurt am M.: Suhrkamp, 1959).

[221]*A Marxist Looks at Jesus* (Philadelphia: Fortress, 1976).

[222]*A Materialist Reading of the Gospel of Mark* (Maryknoll, N.Y.: Orbis, 1981) 241–97.

[223]*Faith in History and Society: Toward a Practical Fundamental Theology* (New York: Seabury, 1980); *The Emergent Church: The Future of Christianity in a Postbourgeois World* (New York: Crossroad, 1981). Cf. J. B. Metz, K. Rahner, and M. Machoveč, *Can a Christian Be a Marxist?* (Chicago: Argus, 1969).

falsifies it, since it reduces the "Christ of faith" merely to a principle of hope or to a "mythologization" of his historical personage. Jesus and his "praxis" have thus become a "model" from the past, and they are now invoked to sanction the use of questionable means (1.2.9.3). Since Jesus' relation to the work of the Spirit in the Church is scarcely considered, such a Christology runs the risk of becoming a mere anthropology.

APPROACH 10:
SYSTEMATIC CHRISTOLOGIES OF A NEW SORT

Under this heading the Commission groups the Christological studies of the Reformed theologian K. Barth and the Catholic littérateur H. U. von Balthasar. It sees both of them as examples of "a *theo*-logical revelation of God Himself" (1.1.10.1). They are Christologies that use the Bible in a somewhat critical way, but also seek to cope with the contribution of the entire Bible to their systematic syntheses. The Jesus of history and the Christ of faith are not opposed but are joined to explain how Jesus Christ is the self-revelation of God in human history.

Barth's starting point is multiple and includes a view of Holy Writ as prophetic and basic to his synthesis, of God as a supreme and transcendent being, of human reasoning as absolutely incapable of knowing Him (because of its perversion in the Fall), and of the uselessness of religious experience (as understood by Schleiermacher and the Hegelians). God has revealed Himself in Jesus Christ, and this Word of God is His sole means of communication with human beings, who come to know Him only in faith under grace.[224] Under the guidance of the Spirit, the Word of God is proclaimed in the Church, and the Word and faith meet in a personal encounter, confirmed in sacraments. The many facets of Barth's theology (e.g. his teaching on the Trinity, grace, justification, the Holy Spirit, the Church, politics, and society) are all ultimately traced to his doctrine of the Word of God, developed under four headings: (1) the Word of God as the criterion of dogmatics; (2) as the rev-

---

[224]*Church Dogmatics, Volume I: The Doctrine of the Word of God, Parts 1 and 2* (Edinburgh: Clark, 1932). Cf. *Dogmatics in Outline* (New York: Harper & Row, 1959; orig., 1946); H. U. von Balthasar, *The Theology of Karl Barth* (New York: Holt, Rinehart and Winston, 1971).

elation of God (triune, incarnate, poured out as the Spirit); (3) as Holy
Scripture; and (4) as the proclamation of the Church.

Greatly influenced by Barth's theology, H. U. von Balthasar developed his own "esthetic" understanding of Christology.[225] Jesus
Christ is the only human being in history who dared claim that God had
established him in the OT and who was hence regarded as crazy (Mk
3:21) and ultimately put to death on the cross. Yet God confirmed that
claim by raising him from the dead. That same God also eternally "defined" him, "You are my beloved Son," in sending him on a unique
and universal mission; his received divinity is not a sharing of God with
a creature, but a giving over of divinity to one who is God (*Deum de
Deo*).[226] Jesus lives his human consciousness completely as a sending;
in the Holy Spirit he has the commission from the Father to reveal the
reality of God and His salvific dealings with human beings. Jesus' whole
existence, even in his "sufferings" (*pathē*), stands in the service of his
proclamation of God—not to manifest himself as the greatest example
of humanity, but solely to carry out the will of the Father. The sending
of which Jesus is conscious is the sending of the only Son; as one sent,
he is the single unit who abides in time as the eternal one. One can call
it his *kenōsis,* as in Philippians 2, but this affirms no mythological al-
teration in God, but only that the Son who has all from the Father "leaves
behind" his *Gottgestalt (morphē theou)* with the Father (1.1.10.1).[227]

The Christological syntheses of both Barth and Balthasar are professedly less tied to critical hypothesis in NT study, but they tend to sacrifice the variety of the NT Christologies to their ideally conceived
syntheses and tend to belittle some of the preparatory elements in OT
theology that have to be considered in any proper study of the totality of
the mystery of Christ, for those elements too form part of the divine pedagogy (1.2.10).[228] But they quote Scripture to their purposes.

---

[225]*The Glory of the Lord: A Theological Aesthetics* (Edinburgh: Clark, 1982); *Herr-
lichkeit: Eine theologische Aesthetik* (3 vols. in 5 tomes; Einsiedeln: Johannes-V., 1961–
69); "Christi Sendung und Person," *Theodramatik, 2/2: Die Personen in Christus* (Einsiedeln: Johannes-V., 1978) 136–238, esp. 206–9.
[226]Ibid. 190.
[227]Ibid. 209.
[228]The Commission notes that it is using "pedagogy" in a sense different from the
use of it in Gal 3:24. There Paul speaks of humanity before Christ being like a child in its
minority "kept under restraint" by a "custodian" (*paidagōgos,* lit. "boy-leader"), i.e.

APPROACH 11:
CHRISTOLOGIES "FROM ABOVE" AND CHRISTOLOGIES "FROM BELOW"

This category is not really separate from some of the approaches already discussed, since several of them could also be so described as one or the other. A Christology "from above" (or a descent Christology) is a title for an approach that either uses the traditional explanation of Jesus Christ as the God-man (especially in its Chalcedonian formulation) or uses the Incarnation as its starting point. A Christology "from below" (or an ascent Christology) begins rather with the Gospel data about Jesus of Nazareth in his earthly ministry and moves to an acknowledgment of him as Lord and Son of God. Neither term is per se negative or pejorative; it merely describes the thrust of the approach used.

The Commission notes that a number of contemporary exegetes and theologians combine both of these aspects, in that they admit an "implicit Christology" as already present in the words and conduct of Jesus of Nazareth, which forms a continuum with the varied explicit Christologies that came to be formulated about him in the Gospels and other NT writings—a continuum that is not always explained in the same way.[229] The Commission finds two things to be common in the different explanations: (1) A distinction is made between the way Jesus of Nazareth presented himself to his contemporaries or was understood by them

---

the slave attendant of the minor child, charged to keep the young boy in tow, superintend his conduct, and see that he did his duties, scholastic and otherwise. The child was under such a disciplinarian until it came of age, until "the time set by the father" (Gal 4:2). See further *JBC*, art. 49, §24–25.

[229] In this regard the Commission mentions the following writers, who have diverse explanations of the continuum: L. Bouyer (*The Eternal Son: A Theology of the Word of God and Christology* [Huntingdon, Ind.: Our Sunday Visitor, 1978]); R. H. Fuller (*The Foundations of New Testament Christology* [New York: Scribner's, 1965]); C. F. D. Moule (*The Origin of Christology* [Cambridge: University Press, 1977]); I. H. Marshall (*The Origins of New Testament Christology* [London: Inter-Varsity, 1977]); (*I Believe in the Historical Jesus* [Grand Rapids, Mich.: Eerdmans, 1977]); C. Duquoc (*Christologie: Essai dogmatique: L'Homme Jésus* [Paris: Cerf, 1968]); W. Kasper (*Jesus the Christ* [New York: Paulist, 1976]); M. Hengel (*The Son of God: The Origin of Christology and the History of Jewish-Hellenistic Religion* [Philadelphia: Fortress, 1976]); J. D. G. Dunn (*Christology in the Making: A New Testament Inquiry into the Origins of the Doctrine of the Incarnation* [Philadelphia: Westminster, 1980]).

and the way his followers came to believe in him after the resurrection. Though a radical interruption or break between these two ways is denied, an advance over the earlier impression or a transformation of the earlier understanding is regarded as constitutive of explicit Christology. The limits of the humanity of Jesus of Nazareth are not pressed to exclude an acknowledgment of Christian faith aroused by his resurrection and his Spirit. (2) When OT titles and roles are predicated of Jesus in the NT and are said to be fulfilled in him, an amplification of the meaning of them that goes beyond that of the OT itself or even of contemporary Palestinian Jewish interpretation has to be noted. This amplification is not simply derived from secondary theological speculation, but is rooted in the person of Jesus himself, whose characteristics are thus set in a better light (1.1.11.2a-b).

The Commission finds that such exegetes and theologians admit that Jesus' individual personality was shaped by his Jewish culture and education and attribute to him a ''quite singular consciousness of himself'' (1.1.11.3), which concerned his relation to God and to his salvific mission on behalf of humanity—a consciousness that grew or developed (Lk 2:40, 52). But these scholars hesitate to psychoanalyze Jesus of Nazareth, aware of the ''critical problems in the texts'' (composed at least a generation after his death and resurrection) and of the dangers of excessive or defective speculation. As an example of the critical problems, one could easily cite the difference between the way the Synoptic Jesus speaks and that of the Johannine Jesus—the former with many isolated sayings and (prophetic, legal, sapiential, minatory) pronouncements (or apophthegms), and many parables, whereas the latter uses long discourses (dialogues becoming monologues), symbolic and absolute ''I am'' sayings, and scarcely any parables. For such reasons these exegetes and theologians prefer to be circumspect about what the Commission calls ''the mystery of his personality,'' since Jesus himself apparently did not take the pains to define it more precisely for his contemporaries.[230]

Finally, the Commission commends the attempts of these modern

---

[230]The Commission mentions H. Schürmann as an interpreter of the NT who holds that the Jesus of history did accord ''a mere glimpse'' into the secrets of his intimate being; see his article ''Die vorösterlichen Anfänge der Logientradition,'' *Traditionsgeschichtliche Untersuchungen zu den synoptischen Evangelien* (Düsseldorf: Patmos, 1968) 37–65.

scholars who join soteriology with Christology, since the purpose of the Word becoming flesh (Jn 1:14) was precisely to be a mediator between God and humanity. What is striking is that the Commission seems to admit that questions about the knowledge and pre-existence of Jesus, unavoidable though they may be, belong not to the "implicit" Christology of the earthly Jesus but to "a late stage of Christology" (1.1.11.4), unless that statement is to be understood as a reflection of the views of the exegetes and theologians. In any case, the Commission, while commending the efforts of such scholars to unite a Christology "from below" with one "from above," notes that certain questions are still without adequate answers: the critical questions about the Gospels (1.2.11.1), the relation of Christology to the whole Bible and to Jewish culture studied against the background of archeological and ethnological discoveries, and also the question of Jesus' pre-existence as the Word and Wisdom of God. Better Scripture studies are needed to probe the relation of the risen Christ to the Spirit and to the Church.

In section 3 the Commission, having considered and criticized various aspects of eleven different modern approaches to Christology, proceeds to ask how the risks, limitations, and ambiguities found in them can be avoided. The Commission's answer appeals to "the principle of totality," i.e. that in the study of Christology one has to listen to the whole of the biblical tradition, the OT as well as the NT, since it is all given to us as the norm of Christian faith (1.3.1–2). Indeed, the literary development in the canonical unity of the Bible reflects the progressive revelation of God and His salvation offered to human beings. One must trace, then, the promises made to the patriarchs and subsequently expanded through the prophets, the expectations of God's kingdom and Messiah that these have both introduced, and finally the realization of them in Jesus of Nazareth as the Messiah and Son of God. This principle of totality the Commission links with the Church's entire tradition and solidarity in faith, as well as with the teaching of the Fathers and medieval theologians—even though both of these groups of interpreters read the Bible in the unsophisticated modes of their times.

Striking, indeed, is the Commission's next comment (1.3.3) that such an "integral Christology," based on the whole Bible, must be "conducted with the aid of the exegetical methods of our age." These same studies must, moreover, "become more advanced in research and investigation than they are at present.'' Lest anyone try to read such a comment as a condemnation of the so-called historical-critical method, the Commission makes it clear that the contrary is meant:

> Indeed, many problems still remain obscure about the composition process of the sacred writings that finally emerged from their inspired authors. As a result, those who would dispense with the study of the problems of this sort would be approaching Scripture only in a superficial way; wrongly judging that their way of reading Scripture is "theological," they would be setting off on a deceptive route. Solutions that are too easy can in no way provide the solid basis needed for studies in biblical theology, even when engaged in with full faith (1.3.3).[231]

Having stated the "principle of totality" and its view of what an "integral Christology" should consist of, the Commission proceeds in Part II to sketch the global testimony of Scripture to Christ. This part of the document needs little commentary, since it merely sets forth in two sections the promises and expectations of salvation and a savior in the OT, and the fulfilment of these promises and expectations in the person of Jesus of Nazareth in the NT.

Section 1, in describing the OT teaching about God's salvific activity on behalf of His people and the emergence of a messianic expectation in Israel, concentrates on three aspects of OT theology: (1) Israel's knowledge of Yahweh as the one, true God, distinct from all others, and as the one who sought out and chose a people for Himself (2.1.1); (2) Israel's experience of Yahweh's salvific will, promises, and covenant with it (2.1.2); and (3) Israel's experience of the various ways that Yah-

---

[231]In 1.3.1 F has "le théologien," whereas L has "peritos in re biblica." Since what is recommended should be taken for granted among biblical interpreters, the French form of the text is undoubtedly more correct.—In speaking of the speculative Christological syntheses of Barth and Balthasar (1.2.10), the Commission commends their disinclination to depend on "critical hypotheses." But it also expresses the desideratum that "exegetical studies may find a more precise and well-defined place in this study of revelation" (engaged in by Barth and Balthasar). It should be noted that the Commission's comment in 1.3.3 runs counter to much of the ranting of Balthasar against "modern exegesis" (see his article "Exegese und Dogmatik," *Internationale katholische Zeitschrift* 5 [1976] 385–92).

weh used to mediate His salvation to it—through kings, priests, prophets, and sages (2.1.3.1). Yet Israel's backsliding experience disclosed in time that such forms of mediation proved inadequate for an abiding mode of communion with God; so Yahweh stirred up in Israel the hope of new mediators: a King-Messiah,[232] a Servant of Yahweh, and a Son of Man. He also expressed His creative and salvific presence to Israel through certain "figurative powers," the Spirit of God, the Word of God, and the Wisdom of God. Section 1 ends with a description of various ways in which Palestinian Jews of the last pre-Christian centuries lived with these expectations of the Messiah(s) and the kingdom of God (2.1.4), concluding with the preaching of John the Baptist.

Section 2 sketches the fulfilment of the OT promises and expectations in Jesus of Nazareth, "born of a woman, born under the law" (Gal 4:4), in whose person the kingdom has drawn near and is at work among human beings. But the testimony of the NT shows that this fulfilment also brought a qualitative difference—it was not just what the people of Jesus' time expected from their reading of the OT. In this the Commission is not naive, for it notes that the different "testimony of the Gospels" stems from disciples who, though they were witnesses of Jesus' words and deeds, have handed them on to us in varying forms under the inspiration of the Holy Spirit—faithfully, indeed, but with their own "Spirit-inspired reflection," which accounts for their diversity in writing, ideas, and vocabulary (2.2.1.1).

The Commission next comments on the use of titles for Jesus in the NT (Master, Prophet, King, Messiah, Son of David, Son of Man,[233] Suffering Servant, Word, and Wisdom) and shows how the biblical data can be used in a proper Christology "from above" and "from below" (2.2.1.2). But it prefers to call these "two routes for Christology," and they are not to be understood as pitted one against the other.

---

[232]One could wish that more precision had been used in citing OT passages here. Zech 9:9–10 mentions a king (in triumph), but there is no mention of an "anointed one" (*māšîah*). This Old Testament passage is apparently being read in the light of Mt 21:4–5—rightly? Similarly, what has Ps 2:10–12 to do with a messiah? Ps 2:2 might have been more pertinent. Again, Dan 9:25 would have been better cited instead of 2:44–45.

[233]Here too one could wish that a little more precision had been used in the discussion of the title "Son of Man." The Commission merely repeats the view that "Jesus alone uses [this title] of himself in the Gospel texts," with no allowance for the problem of Mk 2:10; Mt 9:6; Lk 5:24. See my comments on it in *The Gospel according to Luke (I–IX)* (AB 28; Garden City, N.Y.: Doubleday, 1981) 579–85.

Still more important is the stress that the Commission puts on the relationship of Jesus of Nazareth to God, his filial relation to *Abba,* based on Mk 13:32; 14:36; Mt 11:25–27; Lk 10:21–22; and Jn 3:35–36; 5:19–23; 17:1. This stress is clearly correct, but one might wish that the Commission had better nuanced and distinguished the Synoptic and Johannine data that bear on this relationship.

In line with the new quest for the historical Jesus and with those interpreters who have been advocating a Christology "from below" joined to one "from above," the Commission firmly establishes the person of Jesus of Nazareth as the origin of Christology: "we see that all the titles, all the roles and mediatory modes related to salvation in Scripture have been assumed and united in the person of Jesus" (2.2.1.4). In him too is to be sought the origin of Christian faith, which is not merely a response to the early Christian kerygma (2.2.2.1). Here the nuances of the Commission's mode of expression are not to be missed. The allegiance that disciples manifested to Jesus during his earthly ministry can be called "faith" (2.2.2.1a), but it "remained very imperfect as long as he was alive." Indeed, it was "completely shattered at his death." Only with the light of Easter was their reaction to him turned into real Christian faith, and not only as a faith in God's kingdom already announced by him but as a faith in Jesus himself. Thus was born a Christology rooted in the "Jesus whom the apostles had known before his death and who by his resurrection from the dead had entered into his glory (Lk 24:26; Acts 2:36)" (2.2.2.1c). Yet such a Christology continued to develop as the gospel tradition itself did, until it was eventually consigned to writing in four different forms or booklets. Next (2.2.2.2b) the Commission refers to its own *Instruction on the Historical Truth of the Gospels,* in which it had distinguished three stages of that tradition: (1) what the Jesus of history did and said (= A.D. 1–33); (2) what the apostles and disciples preached about him and his message (= A.D. 33–65); and (3) what the evangelists recorded as they selected from and synthesized that preaching and explicated it in four different literary compositions (= A.D. 65–95).[234]

The Commission, however, goes still further and instructs the readers of the Gospels to "learn to look for *the Christology of each evan-*

---

[234]See the text of the *Instruction* mentioned in n. 3 above, §§VI–IX.

gelist" (2.2.2.2b), and even of each NT writer. All of them bear witness, indeed, to the same Christ, but "with voices that differ as in the harmony of one piece of music." Hence one is not to prefer the testimony of one author to the exclusion of another: "All these testimonies must be accepted in their totality" (2.2.2.2c).

The Commission terminates its discussion of Christology with several paragraphs devoted to Christ as the mediator of salvation, present in his Church and active through the Spirit, and also to the Total Christ, who is the goal of all creation.

In a sense, there is little that is new in Part II of this document, even though new emphases are given to many of the traditional biblical ideas. It is rather the insistence on the total Christological picture in the Bible that is important. It is, moreover, welcome in view of the often one-sided Christologies that have been proposed in modern times, some of which were surveyed in Part I. Noteworthy indeed is the positive tone of the document, since, even when the risks of some of the approaches were being singled out, the way in which this was done was neither excessive nor overly negative.

BIBLICAL INDEX

INDEX OF MODERN AUTHORS

TOPICAL INDEX

Abba, 45, 81, 95
Abraham, 21, 33–35
Anthropology, theological, 11–13,
    25–27, 75–81, 84
Appearances of the risen Christ, 47,
    74
Archeology, 8, 30, 67

Babylonian Talmud, 66
Behistun, Rock of, 67
Biblical Commission, v, 3, 32, 54,
    and *passim*
    Bible et christologie, v, vii–viii,
      1–2, 54–55
    commentary on, 54–96
    members who worked on text, 54
    translation of, 3–53
    Fede e cultura, 55
    Historical Truth of the Gospels,
      48, 95
    Responsa of early 20th century, 64
Biblical criticism, 4, 16, 19–20, 30–
    32, 56, 91, 93
Biblical theology, 62

Canon of Scripture, 31
Christ of faith, 13, 21, 29, 74, 82, 88
Christ, the total, 52–53, 57, 96
Christology
    amplified or developed, 18, 30,
      42, 47, 94

functional, 10, 72, 75
implicit, 17–19, 30, 90–92
of John, 48
of Paul, 48
of various NT writers, 48
ontological, 10, 72, 75
methodologies or approaches in
    anthropological, 11–13, 25–27,
      75–81
    classical, traditional, 4, 19–20,
      58–60
    esthetic, 16–17, 89
    existentialist, 13–14, 27–28,
      82–85
    from above/from below, 17–19,
      29–30, 78, 90–92, 94
    historically researched, 5–7, 21,
      62–66
    history of religions, 7–8, 22, 66–
      69
    Jewish background, 8–10, 23, 69–
      71
    materialist/Marxist, 14–16, 28–29,
      86–88
    liberation theology, 15–16, 28–29,
      86–88
    new systematic sorts, 16–17, 29,
      88–89
    salvation history, 10–11, 23–25,
      71–75
    sociological, 14–16, 28–30, 85–88